MAKING THE WORLD AUTONOMOUS
A Global Role for the European Union

MAKING THE
WORLD AUTONOMOUS

A Global Role for the European Union

Anthony Clunies-Ross

DUNEDIN ACADEMIC PRESS

Edinburgh

Published by
Dunedin Academic press Ltd
Hudson House
8 Albany Street
Edinburgh EH1 3QB
Scotland

ISBN 1 903765 46 3

British Library Cataloguing in Publication Data
A catalogue record for this book is available from the British Library

Typeset in Plantin
by Makar Publishing Production
Printed in Great Britain by Cromwell Press

I would dedicate this work to all members of my extended family, living or now departed, that I have known; in particular to my father, Ian Clunies-Ross – Australian patriot but also world-citizen, delighting in diversity – because of the visionary concern that he shared with many others around sixty years ago over the institutions needed to build a better world; and in particular also to Kirsty, Laura, and Sean, because they will very probably still be here in sixty years' time, and will be able to judge how far the human family has moved by then towards arrangements that enable it to live with mutual responsibility and forbearance, as I believe it is designed to do.

Contents

Foreword

In international affairs there are so many immediate crises and obstacles that the search for desirable long-term changes in the way the world's affairs are run has almost gone out of fashion. In particular, the phrase 'world government' is taboo.

And yet, fateful developments of many kinds from global warming, to the end of cheap oil, to the proliferation and general availability of nuclear and other weapons of mass destruction, point inexorably to the urgent need for a dramatic improvement in what is politely called 'international governance'.

It is therefore refreshing to read in Anthony Clunies-Ross's new book, a clear-eyed statement of the need to move toward some elements of government at the global level and a practical suggestion of the part the European Union might play in this historic, and very necessary, evolution.

Brian Urquhart
Former Under Secretary-General of the United Nations

Acknowledgements

My sincere thanks to Brian Urquhart for writing a Foreword to this book; to Richard Harries for his encouraging comment; to Anthony Kinahan for all his support as publisher; to Susan Milligan for her careful but also responsive text-editing; and to all my good friends who have kindly read in advance the whole or various parts, either of drafts of this book or of a longer (unpublished) text of which it is in some manner a spin-off, and have offered corrections, suggestions or encouragement. They have of course no responsibility for the outcome, and indeed I know that some have been uneasy about its theme. Beside members of my family – Morag, Sarah, and Brigit – they include: Tony Atkinson, Dauvit Broun, Charles Dundas, Jeremy Heimans, Peter Hill, Bill Inglis, Valerie Inglis, John Langmore, Joyce Leigh, Simon Lockett, Damian O'Sullivan, Roger Perman, Nicholas Ruane, Luc van Liedekerke, David Vines, Harry Wardlaw, Adele Wick, and Rory Williams.

Chapter 1

Introduction: the themes stated

This book is not about predictions. It is about desirable possibilities. Its message is that an outcome with the highest potential for good is actually *possible* – possible, that is, on certain conditions: conditions to whose realization we can contribute. And, once a favourable course of events is widely recognized as possible, its probability of coming to pass is greatly enhanced.

The central paradox to be resolved

There is a monstrous, tragic paradox that has become so familiar that we readily forget it.

Almost all of us want peace so that we and our neighbours can live out our lives and enjoy what the earth and modern technology afford. Most of us, when we come to think of it, would wish to do so with environmental security for our grandchildren and reasonable civil and social justice for the six billion people who share the earth with us.

Yet collectively we have piled up enough weapons to exterminate our whole species many times over.

For sixty years we have been developing nuclear weapons and ways of delivering them. Amazingly, quite large numbers were destroyed in the 1990s. Even so, as Martin Rees writes (2003: 43), whereas the Oklahoma City attack killed 160 people with the equivalent of about three tonnes of TNT, the nuclear stockpiles of the former Soviet Union and the US carry the equivalent to that explosive power *for every person in the world*. There is enough on that arithmetic to destroy 960 billion human lives. The most acute danger, though far from the only one, is that any of the weapons should fall into the hands of gangsters and fanatics.

A non-proliferation treaty was made to cap the number of nuclear powers when there were only five of them. Yet now there are eight or more, and the number seems set to rise. The only military use of the weapons is to create immense slaughter and destruction. Their only responsible use is to deter others from using them. The more weapons of mass destruction there are, and the more numerous the hands that have authorized access to them, the more chance they have of coming into the control of 'unofficials', who may well have far less restraint than the most trigger-happy government.

And nuclear weapons are just the summit of world armaments. There are biological weapons, also of potentially unlimited destructive power; and chemical weapons; and the great variety of conventional weapons, which have after all accounted for almost every act of organized killing that we have seen, even since 1945.

Collectively we know that the path we have been treading is crazy. Most of us – surely the overwhelming majority in every country – do not want to destroy humankind or any part of it. And that is the risk – while the weapons are there, and clever, ingenious fanatics exist, and sovereign states behave as they have traditionally behaved, and some of them are not scrupulous in guarding against every contingency. Collectively we face St Paul's dilemma: 'The good that I would I do not. The evil that I would not, that I do.'

The trouble is that we see no plausible way out. Everyone is holding arms for fear of attack by someone else. We recognize echoes of the preparations that led to the First World War. Every state had, or claimed it had, a good – rational, moral – reason for being highly armed and for fighting. But collectively it was suicide.

There is a device that has emerged to deal with precisely this problem. It is called *government*. The trouble is that it has so far been used to impose peace and order only across subgroups of the human family. In principle we know that the order a government can deliver is needed *across the globe*. Yet we see no way in which this can be done acceptably, or even tolerably: in practice, no way in which it can be done at all.

Yet I shall argue here that there is a process, an expedient, that might eventually solve the dilemma. It could enable us to create – without significant loss – the patterns of incentives, and hence the patterns of behaviour, that we desperately need.

And it is not just a bright idea. It is present in healthy embryo, and we have seen it at work. It does not need much pushing: it has motive power of its own. We simply need to avoid raising obstructions and to direct it. But that means we need a view of the direction. And we need patience because the task may well take decades to complete. It may not be as fast as we should like, yet still be an irreplaceable element in any adequate solution.

The case to be argued

This work has four related themes.

Global governmental organization: a crucial long-term goal

First, it argues that we should be deliberately working now toward *global political or governmental organization*. What is meant by this is a world authority which, within the limits of a constitution, might on certain matters override national governments: on those matters its decisions would have general application and would not be subject to veto by those governments. This can only be a long-term goal: one that we might hope to achieve in thirty or fifty years or even longer. Failing some unthinkable disaster that might upset all calculations, it will come gradually or not at all.

On the other hand, it is a matter of urgency. We must forestall if we can the emergence of a world of three or four or five superpowers reminiscent of 1914. We must establish firm global control of the most dangerous weapons, in order to prevent if possible their acquisition by rogue states or fanatics. And we must establish procedures to reduce the incidence of the kind of political grievances that lead to the emergence of unofficial paramilitaries.

The form of political organization in mind – as not only best in itself but also most likely to be realized – I characterize as a *minimal democratic confederation*. By saying that it is a confederation (rather than a federation) I intend to imply that there will be constitutional processes through which any member-state may withdraw from the association unilaterally. By the word 'minimal' I mean that the central body will *not* have powers over all of the matters that are generally under central control in federal states; its powers will be confined to those that are absolutely necessary for its crucial purposes. By 'democratic' I understand that the authority will be subject (under whatever additional restrictions) to free election – or to an assembly freely elected – in at least rough proportion to population, by all the adult people within its jurisdiction. It must be democratic because there is no other general principle at all likely to command universal support.

There are various compelling reasons why we should be pressing toward this end as fast as may be, given only certain essential conditions on which it can be acceptable. The most urgent reason is the need to maintain peace and to control weapons of mass destruction. But there is also the hazard of environmental disaster and the reality of both appalling oppression and also (physically, logistically, technically) unnecessary extremes of poverty.

At best it is likely to be a long haul. We may be facing half a century or more before the objective, the essential set of institutions, is fully attained. Yet the likely delay, and the many obstacles, are no reason for forgetting the goal – just as commitment to the goal is no reason for failing to seek the best substitutes in the meantime: for preserving peace and safety and the other benefits toward which a global political organization seems ultimately the most or the only effective means.

I shall argue that the goal is not intrinsically utopian and that it should not be approached in a utopian spirit. It is not intrinsically utopian because there are plausible means that we can adopt now for furthering the gradual process of reaching it.

Consensual global governance: as solution and as stopgap

Second, but also of prime importance, we should provide now, as far as possible, within the existing world of largely independent states, for performing the essential functions that a benevolent world authority would be expected to fulfil. This is what is generally meant in current discussion by the term *global governance*. The term 'governance' naturally includes government in the usual sense, but is broader. And the 'global governance' that can be discussed as part of the immediate agenda must work by consensual methods with and through existing governments.

So I shall distinguish *global political or governmental organization* from *consensual global governance*: governmental from consensual arrangements. The line between the two may appear to be a fine one. Both may allow the choices of individual states or nations in certain circumstances to be overridden. And on the other hand governmental arrangements, no less than consensual ones, in the context contemplated here, depend on consent for their formation and continuance. But what is referred to here as consensual global governance is a creature of the governments of its constituting states. It is *their* consent, unanimous in every case or not, that is its ruling principle. That is very different from joint democratic government as we normally understand it – different in principle and different in practice.

These two pursuits – toward global governmental organization, and toward benevolent and effective consensual global governance – are both essential; and neither need conflict – neither must be allowed to conflict – with the other. For some vital purposes, a number of them – such as postal, telecoms, and meteorological co-operation – broadly achieved many years ago, the second is likely to be enough. For others, it is never likely to be more than a stopgap.

Different but complementary paths

Third, these two must largely be sought through separate sets of institutions. Consensual global governance as an immediate objective – to work in the world of states as it is – must come largely through the United Nations family in the broadest sense: associations of governments that aim to be immediately all-inclusive. Global political organization, on the other hand, with its elements of confederal government, must come through the gradual extension and constitutional development, from among existing states, of one or more selective unions with at least embryonic governmental characteristics: of a kind of which the European Union is now by far the most prominent and advanced example.

What follows is that the European Union has a potential function of the utmost importance: a role that is distinct from those most commonly supposed for it. It can be not only the model for transnational political organization but also the vehicle through which political organization on a global scale is approached. In some ways it is well fitted for this task, more so certainly than any other existing institution. But if this is the most important of the possible roles for the EU to play, then there will be implications for how the Union should develop: what constitutional arrangements and assumptions of Union power are helpful and what are not.

In particular, it must decisively abandon the notion, dear to many enthusiasts for the European movement, that any increase in uniformity and in centralized hierarchical power within the Union is a triumph. However much the opposite principle – subsidiarity – is asserted, this idea remains pervasive. It brings the Union into disrepute among many whose support it needs. And it risks making an ever-wider union impossible.

At a time when there is, rightly, talk of the post-modern state and networked government – calling attention to the departures we have recently witnessed from the concepts of sovereignty and hierarchy that are held to have prevailed since the 1648 Treaty of Westphalia – we are in danger of aping a model now two centuries old, the neat North-American-style federation. This in spite of the fact that the reality of the movement for European co-operation, even of the Union itself, has not conformed to that pattern. For very good reasons, it has had more of the adaptive untidiness of post-Franco Spain, or of recent developments in that habitual maverick, the United Kingdom of Great Britain and Northern Ireland: indigenous modern European responses to the challenge of running a democratic multinational state.

Central powers, aspirations to uniformity, must be confined to the minimum necessary.

Urgency of a common foreign and security policy

There is a fourth, subordinate theme, not broached here until Chapter 7. It arises in response to the momentous events of the first four months of 2003, during which this work was being drafted. This is that the particular aspiration of the European Union to a common defence and foreign policy is not only of long-term importance; it is also a matter of some urgency. And it will not happen with existing institutions alone. Through the first six chapters, this theme will be left dormant.

Controversial, but symbiotic, themes

Of the three main thrusts of the argument of the work, the second is widely accepted, implicitly or explicitly, and I shall be concerned less to argue the *need* for consensual global governance than to consider (a) the means for making it more complete and effective, and (b) its likely limits – the limits to its effectiveness – as an alternative to global political organization. It is the first and the third themes of the work that will be controversial.

The broad case for global political or governmental organization is obvious enough and even familiar, but it is conventionally dismissed on the ground that planning or hoping for such an outcome is completely unrealistic: there are no terms on which it could become generally acceptable.

The assertion that European union (or the European Union) should be seen as a seed-crystal from which global political organization might develop is thus subject to two disadvantages. First, it is irrelevant if global political organization itself – democratic world confederation, however limited – is necessarily and only a utopian dream. But second, even among utopians, it seems hardly ever to have been vented. This double burden can make it seem like the elaboration of an outlandish route to an insubstantial goal.

Consequently I have first to argue, against much conventional wisdom, that something with a claim to be considered highly desirable is also possible; and then, from the base of that argument, to put a case that seems rarely if ever to have been publicly advanced about the means to that end.

But not only does the second of these two arguments depend for its relevance on the first. The first also is much strengthened if the second can be made convincing. If we can derive some picture – rooted in what is actually happening – of *how* world political organization might be achieved, the case for contemplating it as a real possibility becomes so much the more compelling.

But is it realistic to plan for world political organization?

To end international wars and to control weapons of mass destruction; to institute universally accepted and routine procedures for seeking resolutions or compromises over grievances of the kinds that lead to insurgencies; to prevent global-scale environmental disasters of human origin; to correct the worst extremes of poverty; and to protect essential human rights: there can be little argument with these objectives. And it may be easy enough to see how they are unlikely to be reliably fulfilled unless there is a constitution through which the lethal powers of states can be pooled and certain decisions can be taken and implemented, by normal democratic political processes, *for the world as a whole*. For the world as a whole: that is, across the various vested interests and prejudices that can associate themselves with the governments of particular states.

We need to make the world as an entity *autonomous*: able to take and implement certain kinds of decision in a coherent way on behalf of the totality of its people – just as a broadly democratic constitution enables a nation such as Japan or South Africa or Sweden or Costa Rica to make decisions, deliberately and acceptably, for its own residents and citizens. Not all of the people in those countries agree with all the decisions taken on their behalf; but the huge majority accept the *processes* by which those decisions are made. In this sense Somalia and Sudan and the 'Democratic Republic' of Congo at the turn of the millennium are *not* autonomous.

It is easy to see why reaching that point is no easy task. But an argument commonly heard is that world political organization – turning the world, as the entities that we now regard as 'nations' have been turned, into a decision-maker on its own behalf – is impossible altogether and for ever: 'inconceivable' if the debater wants to make the impossibility sound even more impossible.

There is a ragbag of arguments. People have always fought one another; it is part of human nature. We all have a tribal instinct. There have always been warring nations. Governments will never give up power. People will always distrust foreigners. Political cultures differ from nation to nation. And so on.

It is inconceivable . . .

'It is inconceivable that the kingdoms in England will ever unite into a single realm', as a thoughtful East Anglian or Northumbrian might have said in AD 600. 'It is inconceivable that civilized people should live without slaves', as no doubt many people thought in the Graeco-Roman world. The highly intellectual British Prime Minister, Lord Melbourne, gave something very like this as a reason why he might have or should have opposed the abolition of slavery (Cecil 1955: 151). 'European union is inconceivable because the French and the Germans have always fought each other', as might well have seemed obvious in 1871 or 1919 or 1945. 'It is inconceivable that Hungary or Poland should be allowed to join NATO; it is inconceivable that the Baltic states should become independent again', as seemed only too clear to all right-thinking people as late as 1985. (Hands up who thought otherwise!)

It is certainly unusual for the inconceivable not only to become conceivable but actually to happen in the space of ten or fifteen years. But the extreme case of the events of 1989 to 1992 should surely make us wary of judging anything – especially anything obviously desirable, of gain to all or almost all – as politically impossible. In such cases, never say never.

And most of the generalizations used to give a 'never' verdict in this case are easily seen to be either false (governments *have* given up power, for example) or irrelevant (the fact that there have always been some people who will pick fights does not mean that the lethally armed states that happen through various historical accidents to exist at the present are predestined always to exist in that form and always to fight one another).

Maybe, but not in any future near enough to be worth considering . . .

Practical people consider only those possible future events that may take place within – what, ten years, twenty years – or do they? I have seen plenty of projections of global warming up to the end of the twenty-first century, and projections of the burden of pensions and dependency up to 2040 or 2050. Why? After all, the mortal components of those now planning will be mostly dust and ashes by 2050, and all of them will be away by 2100. But strange as it may seem, the most practical people do feel some care, and take some responsibility, for the generations that will come after. They do not like the idea that their children, or other people's children or grandchildren, will suffer – that the world will suffer – for lack of their own attention to developments which they could and should have foreseen.

Why not leave the future to take care of its own problems?

Why not just wait until the disasters are evident rather than becoming agitated over long-term projections? With both global warming and pensions the reasons are obvious. Decisions taken now, and at every point in between, will closely limit what is possible in 2050 or 2100.

The effects of the human-made processes leading to global warming are cumulative. If acts undertaken in the intervening years have led to evidently disastrous results, the effects cannot just be cancelled by turning off a switch. It may take another century of the most stringent measures to reverse the process that has led to the rise in temperature, and many of the side-effects may well be irreversible.

It is similar with pensions. Once it is clear that the burden of existing arrangements has become intolerable, contracts will have been made; laws will have been passed; expectations will have been built up;

which will combine to make a quick reversal either simply impossible or else so hurtful (to those required to surrender what they have seen as their rights) that society will at best be riven by resentment.

With world political organization, there may be similar problems attending a lack of long-term thinking. We may become locked in the meantime into more exclusive unions. We may find ourselves looking for security to a pair of rival blocs, as over the Cold War time. Or we may find ourselves in an inflammable system of alliances and half-alliances as in 1914. But even if we find a way of escaping such risky conjunctures, a workable and universal union is likely to come only gradually. It will be necessary to show on the ground that one step is tolerable or even beneficial before we move on to the next. And some body of people is likely to need a vision of the goal if movement is to be continuous and in the right direction.

However far away this target may seem, there is a strong case – unless it is judged as forever impossible – to start *now* devising a strategy for achieving it.

Necessary character of the strategy for getting there

That strategy will probably have to imitate in some degree the one adopted by the European movement over the last half-century: starting with a handful of countries and a few shared powers and functions, and then progressively *widening* and *deepening*: admitting those who want to enter and who fulfil the necessary conditions for getting along with the existing members; and expanding either the range of common activities or the extent to which decisions about them are made through genuinely common institutions.

But if this process is to be directed to the goal of a world organization – equipped to define acceptably, and to pursue, the common interests of the human family – there are plenty of potential false turns that will have to be avoided. The members will have to refrain from applying entry conditions, or requiring entrants to engage in common activities, that are irrelevant to the crucial purposes of the union and are likely to exclude certain countries, or to constrain them unduly, for irrelevant reasons.

My contention is that the European Union has already travelled some distance along this road. It has made some false moves and may easily make others. But the false moves are not irreversible, and there are elements in its situation tending to drive it in the right direction. What it needs is a strong segment of people within it that are committed to the wider goal.

Plan of the book

The following are the main questions to be considered.

First (Chapter 2): why world political organization in the sense proposed is necessary, and the case for thinking that it may eventually be possible.

Then (Chapter 3): the choice between consensual and governmental elements in the common institutions for fulfilling various essential global functions; why some governmental powers are necessary globally and some are not; which are the essential subjects for governmental powers; the choice between confederal and federal union.

Next (Chapter 4): why the European Union is a vehicle ready to hand for gradually bringing the necessary global governmental organization to birth; its appeal to outsiders; the capacity of its gateway conditions for raising standards among postulants; the advantages of its untidy character; but also the need to define (sparingly) an essential core of common functions in which all members must join.

Further, at the same time (Chapter 5): the essential role of the institutions of the UN family (including the Washington multilaterals) in current global governance; the advantages and drawbacks of their comprehensive membership; how the role of the UN family can be expanded and modified to make it more effective in promoting common security and justice and its moral authority stronger (peacekeeping and peace-enforcement, recognizing and limiting humanitarian intervention, voluntary tribunals and arbitration, two-way bargains between rich and poor states, global sources of finance).

After that (Chapter 6): the basic constitutional choices for a minimal democratic global confederation – election by governments or populace; checks on the majority; provisions against deadlock; choice among democratic models; rights to secede – and the implications of all of them for the development of the European Union. An Appendix considers the bearing on the objectives espoused in the book of the constitutional proposals for the EU made by the Inter-Governmental Conference that reported in June 2004.

Penultimately (Chapter 7): possible paths from here to there; the particular case for a common EU defence and foreign policy as a matter of urgency; critical steps and possible sequences in widening and deepening.

Chapter 8 summarizes the argument and invites challenges to it.

Chapter 2

World political organization: necessary, possible?

The one hope that we have to prevent this competition from ending
in a terrible effort of mutual destruction . . . is that the Powers may
gradually be brought together, to act together on a friendly spirit
on all questions of difficulty which may arise, until at last they shall
be welded in some international constitution which shall give to the
world as a result of their great strength a long spell of unfettered trade
and continued peace. (Lord Salisbury, speaking as British Prime
Minister at the Guildhall, 1897. Quoted Roberts 2000: 686)

The case for government is also the case for elements of *world* government

The essential reason for wanting global political organization – a form
of world government, however limited – is the same as the reason for
wanting government at all: that there are benefits which we all in a
fashion desire or need but which we cannot reliably enjoy if each of us
makes all decisions independently; and that, in important cases, agreements designed to realize specific benefits will be difficult to reach
through bargaining case by case, and, if reached, will be likely, in the
absence of enforcement, to be infringed.

We need laws to settle disputes among states so as to prevent them
from fighting and plundering and oppressing each other, just as we need
laws to settle disputes among individuals for the same purpose; and it is
difficult to establish a rule of law without an enforcer. There is a body
of public international law that most nations to a degree acknowledge,
but it does not effectively prevent the outbreak of wars between governments. While there are national armies, and no international force to
outweigh them – while there is no recognized international tribunal and

legislature whose decisions cannot be ignored – force and the threat of force will be used by one nation or government against another.

Modern weaponry means that a war pursued on the most apparently just pretext can be enormously destructive of life and livelihood. And a threat of force issued without the slightest desire for actual war may nevertheless lead to precisely that – because of the way internal politics works and because of the perceived need not to lose face or reputation.

What we have learned about the Cuban missile crisis of 1962 from the 'Kennedy tapes' and reminiscences of people near to the action has made it clear that the world was then very close to nuclear war, which, to put it mildly, no one wanted. So far from acting on sober judgement and full information, the superpowers could be ludicrously capricious and ill-informed. Khrushchev appears to have put the missiles in Cuba on a whim without serious political consultation. And, contrary to what the American generals understandably believed, the Soviet commander in Cuba had been authorized to fire his tactical missiles without reference to Moscow.[1] The Americans (according to Robert McNamara, Defense Secretary in 1962) were deliberating on the basis of huge underestimation of the operational state of the missiles in Cuba. There was nothing remotely resembling a direct line between the White House and the Kremlin: at one crucial point Khrushchev had to communicate with Kennedy through a broadcast on Moscow Radio. If Kennedy had not stuck to a line of moderation (against the persistent advice of the Chiefs of Staff and the bullying of some leading members of Congress), or if Khrushchev (subjected to similar pressures from his generals) had not been prepared in the end to climb down, the worst nightmares for the peoples of the Americas, the Soviet Union, and Europe might easily have been realized.

If the superpowers, with some years' experience at that time of the nuclear stand-off, could act on caprice and ignorance in the most dangerous matters, what can we expect of states such as North Korea? What of India and Pakistan – rivals that have much more recently become a nuclear-armed pair – facing popular pressures to provocative action such as neither the USSR nor the USA had to deal with in 1962? President Musharraf (*The Times*, 31.12.2002: 15) indicated in 2002 that earlier in that year he had threatened nuclear retaliation if 'Indian troops moved a single step over the international border or Line of Control'. India's Army chief said that such threats would have made no difference. If both the threat and India's alleged readiness to ignore it were genuine, then nuclear war might easily have been joined. What of all the powers that might acquire nuclear (let alone biological or chemical) weapons in the next few decades?

The lesson of the Cuban crisis, according to Robert McNamara (as recorded by Knightley and Pringle 1992) was as follows: 'The combination of human fallibility and nuclear warheads carry over an extended period of time the near certainty of a nuclear exchange which will destroy nations and threaten our civilisation. The world must move back to a non-nuclear age and we are not on that course today.' Yet nuclear weapons cannot be disinvented, only controlled – either through the existence of a single global body with all necessary authority to control them and whatever might contribute to their production, or by putting an end to war and the risk and fear of war.

But how? The mechanisms of the UN, which have been in operation for over half a century, are of themselves inadequate to ensure that wars (albeit often unintended and undesired by governments on both sides) do not break out or are quickly ended. They are unable either to impose conditions sufficiently acceptable to all sides of a dispute or to restrain aggressive action. For the formal enforcement procedures to come into play at all requires at least the passive consent of all five Permanent Members of the Security Council. And then their capacity to impose a settlement depends on (a) voluntary compliance on the part of the states in dispute (Article 40 of the Charter), or (b) economic or communication or symbolic sanctions (Article 41), which have often proved ineffective, or (c) military action under UN auspices (Article 42). No active military intervention – nothing designed to defeat an antagonist in battle – was authorized between 1950 and 1990–1. UN peacekeeping in practice, though often most valuable, has been extremely modest in scale and generally supposed a pre-existing truce.

Law for dispute-settlement voluntarily and universally observed by a population of independent armed states is not inconceivable – in the strict sense of being conceptually contradictory – and attempts to approach it may well be valuable. (Ways of improving the prospects along those lines will be suggested in Chapter 5.) But, as the only strategy ever for preventing interstate war, it is unpromising. While states make a point of having independent foreign policies and devoting significant proportions of their peoples' substance to military preparations, it is always likely that influential members of their constituencies will expect them to act as armed independent states have traditionally acted – forcefully, heroically – that is, in a way that overrides calculations of safety and material benefit: safety and material benefit even for their own people, let alone for the rest of the world.

So it is difficult to see how the half-century-old Israel–Palestine conflict can be satisfactorily settled except under generally accepted enforced impartial law, or at least an element of strong co-ordinated external pressure – whatever the role that mediation and conciliation may also have to play. And that conflict is the source of so much else: the wider enmity between the Arab states and Israel, and the pervasive unofficial hostility in Muslim countries to 'the West', especially the United States, that hostility itself the mainspring of the 'global terrorism' whose elimination suddenly became a worldwide cause when it hit America so hard in September 2001.

Unless it can be plausibly argued that a world without independent armed states is necessarily or probably worse than the one we have, or is necessarily impossible ever to achieve, or that the attempt to achieve it would probably block more promising ways of providing for peace and security, it seems irresponsible not to address the possibility seriously.

Alternative strategies: is any of them a path to secure peace?

A righteous hyperpower with overwhelming strength

A vision of world order, now popular in certain circles in the US, is that one power, which acts only on right motives – in the sole interests of freedom and justice, or because its own interests happen to coincide with the demands of freedom and justice for the world – should become more powerful than the others put together and therefore be able to ensure that right is observed and all dangerous disputes justly settled. A number of Americans, used to thinking of their country as a beacon for the world, and realizing that it is now militarily overwhelming, see these two circumstances combined as providing the best solution. Rather than restricting its own action by tying its decisions to the approval of a wicked and divided world, the US should use its own judgement to defend itself in the most direct way possible. This may well involve overthrowing evil regimes everywhere, so giving the rest of the world its best hope of peace and freedom. Many Europeans and Japanese and Australasians, used to having the US as a heavyweight protector during the Cold War, also find its present power reassuring. They may see their best safeguard in simply following its lead.

Others across the world, however, are less happy to submit without appeal to American official motives, values, and judgement. And, even from a purely Stateside view, there are three reasons why the solution is defective.

First, overwhelming military might does not guarantee a country against unofficial action. For this purpose subtler methods may provide the best hope. After the Twin Towers attack, there has been a psychological need for the country to use its great power in some way that gives the convincing impression of punishing such action or deterring its repetition. Yet that way has not been easy to find, and some would say that scapegoats have been selected instead. The people who make the attacks are not calculating the risks for themselves; they often go into action expecting to die. Clever controls may block them. But no weapon in a superpower's arsenal will deter them. On the contrary, strong-arm responses, that inevitably kill and maim and impoverish and humiliate, often unselectively, are likely to be potent recruiting agents for those who plot the revenge of the weak. And, as US experience of 2001–4 shows, intervening to set a country right may involve the intervenor, however powerful, in painful dilemmas. Neither Afghanistan nor Iraq shows unmistakable signs in mid-2004 of emerging as a peaceful democracy.

Second, the existence of weapons of mass destruction (WMDs) reduces the political advantage of superior fire-power. In any near future, Iran or North Korea will always be a midget compared to the US. But, if either of them had even a small arsenal of nuclear weapons and means of delivery, it could not simply be ignored. The US could do much more damage to North Korea than North Korea could do to the US or its allies. Rational calculation with the interests of its people as the criterion would lead a nuclear-armed North Korea to avoid any possibility of war with the US at almost all costs. But who can be sure that these are the considerations that would prevail? Even in advance of possible war with Iraq in 2003, a war whose advocates defended it in part by the need to prevent that nuclear situation from arising, there were fears that Saddam might use the biological and chemical weapons he was then widely believed to have – in revenge if for no other reason – regardless of implied American threats of nuclear retaliation. Samson in Gaza, Hitler in the Berlin bunker: fighting to the last, revenge when all else fails, are familiar enough responses. Where the weaker power can inflict immense damage, which no action on the part of the much stronger power can reliably prevent, the effective advantage of the stronger becomes greatly reduced. And, when there is distrust and opposition between the stronger and the weaker, and the weaker is not quite so weak in relation to the stronger as Iran or North Korea will be in relation to the US over the foreseeable future, there remain the risks of nuclear war by political or technical accident, risks that were sometimes acute, and never went away, during the Cold War confrontation. And, unless any attempt at development of nuclear weapons – or of any WMDs – other than by say the US, Russia, China, Britain, France, Israel, India, and Pakistan, is henceforth to be declared a crime punishable by invasion and regime-change, there may soon be plenty of takers. The more governments feel themselves at a disadvantage in relation to others with WMDs, and the more they sense that the hyperpower – with the best motives, of course – can otherwise dispose of them as it sees fit, the more attractive the nuclear or WMD option may appear.

There is a third worry for a hyperpower that fails to foster international rules and orderly processes but rather relies on acting at its own discretion without regard to interest and opinion in the rest of the world. Its supremacy may come to an end. China has nearly five times the population of the US. On a purchasing-power-parity (PPP) basis of estimation, its total income is about half as large. Its growth rate of income has been – for decades now – much higher. Suppose an 8 per cent growth rate for China and a 3 per cent growth rate for the US between 1998 and 2020, applied to the aggregates that the World Bank gives for 1998 (World Bank 2000: 230–1). By the end of that time, China's total income would be more than a third higher than that of the US. PPP figures may perhaps not be the most appropriate for assessing potential military capacity. With the same rates of growth on conventional exchange-rate-based figures, China would have only a third of the economic weight of the US in 2020, as compared with about an eighth in 1998. But China may continue with a high concentration of spending for military purposes. It is also worth noting from the same source (ibid.: 266–7) that over 1985–95 the number of scientists and engineers in China working in research and development per million people is given as about one-eleventh of that for the US. With nearly five times as many people in total, however, the absolute number would be nearly half as large – and that was in a period centred on 1990. China's aggregate technical capacity by 2020, thirty years later, is likely to be huge. Those who train China's technical and scientific students abroad do not doubt their quality. Given a continuing desire to catch up militarily, it seems not impossible that by that date China will be in the same league as the US. India could on similar calculations also be a considerable military power then. And Russia, itself rated a superpower such a short while ago and still possessed no doubt of a vast reservoir of suitably trained and experienced technical manpower, might well have returned to the front rank. In 2020, then, there might be two to five frontline powers, all nuclear-armed and with the most modern delivery systems, possibly linked in a couple of firm or not-so-firm alliances, or possibly as relatively loose cannon.

The US – and the West, which has relied so much on American hegemony – may then be seen to have two options. One is to strain every sinew in order to keep ahead, so that the US, or the US plus a reasonably united Europe, could 'face', and match if necessary, say, the other three major powers together. This, if successful, would not preclude 1914-type risks: of uncertainty about the firmness of alliances and the possibility of surprise. It would also not preclude Cold-War-type risks: of accidental war, either through technical slips or because the other side's reaction to certain possible moves is miscalculated (the Cuban missile case, probably also the Korean War case). If actual war between members of the top five-or-so happened, it would be an unmitigated disaster, almost certainly extending well beyond the belligerent countries. Given four or five more-or-less-coequal superpowers, diplomacy, with the mistakes of the twentieth century in mind, would need to work at full stretch if peace were to be kept.

If there is no permanently safe stronghold to be gained from trailing in the wake of a righteous hyperpower, what options are left?

The 'New Realism'

One possibility is what Philip Bobbitt (2002: 258–64) calls the 'New Realism'. This is the approach that he associates with Henry Kissinger's writings on diplomacy: one that recognizes the system of states as an arena of competing interests in which the best hope is to find a stable accommodation among them. The traditional quest for a balance of power seeks above all stability, with no one power, and no firm coalition, markedly stronger than the rest. The vital interests of each power need to be respected, and these interests require it not to be left at the mercy of any other. Alliances are justified as a way of preventing this from happening, but for the same reason alliances must be restrained and flexible. Opportunities of negotiation must be kept open.

There is a system to be maintained, one that depends on the primacy of these unwritten rules. Motives irrelevant to this requirement, such as moral outrage, utopian ideology, or legalism (in a sphere in which no law can be enforced), or the pursuit of any particular social objective, are likely to be distractions. The peace preserved in Europe for nearly forty years after the Congress of Vienna of 1814–15 is an example cited by Kissinger (1995: ch. 4) of a successfully maintained balance of power.

The difficulty with this prescription, as Kissinger acknowledges, is that, if it is to be a solution, most of the powers must play the game with something like the same understanding of the rules. They must be broadly content and must not give a high priority to other objectives over the demands of stability. It takes only one maverick to upset the balance. In Kissinger's own view, the Vienna system depended on a common set of assumptions and values; it required a general acceptance of the *status quo*. As I read Kissinger, Napoleon III or Bismarck, neither of them satisfied with the distribution of power that existed, would each have sufficed to destroy the equilibrium of the 1815 settlement (ibid.: ch. 5). Then in 1914, it might be argued, after another longish period of peace among the large European powers that followed the 1878 Congress of Berlin, the players took different views of the relative strength of each of them and of how this was likely to change; emotional allegiances and lingering desires (or fears of others' desires) to reverse pre-1878 defeats or other humiliations affected policies; and enough of Austria's leaders, at least, wanted a war (if only a small one) to tame the Serbs. In retrospect we realize the dangers. But elements such as these, that will interfere with any rational attempt to achieve and preserve a balance, are always likely to be with us. Kissinger regards American moralism, in its various manifestations, as having often confused American diplomacy, but recognizes that American politicians cannot ignore in their policy these firmly rooted tendencies among the people they represent. Dispassionate realism – a readiness to negotiate with longstanding enemies or to form alliances with monsters – may not be easy to maintain.

In the twenty-first century, when the objective realities of relative military strength are likely to change quite quickly, when popular feeling intrudes heavily on foreign policy, and when major powers are only too likely to have a sense of past or present humiliation, reliance on a balance of power alone seems risky.

Partial collective security

Differing from the model of the post-Vienna balance of power is a long-term alliance of the kind exemplified by NATO, the North Atlantic Treaty Organization, in which the members foresee a common and continuing threat and organize to act jointly against it wherever it strikes.

During the Cold War period, America and the West saw the main threat to themselves as coming from the Communist powers and, under US leadership, formed alliances of mutual defence. Of the three regional alliances, the Central Treaty Organization vanished without trace. The South East Asia Treaty Organization was dissolved in 1977 (*Keesing*: 28514), though the 1954 Collective Defence Treaty that it existed to support persisted, but effectively just as a US guarantee to Thailand and the Philippines. Yet NATO, with its co-ordinated military command, appears in retrospect successful. None of its members was subjected to attack in the manner feared, and the Soviet threat as originally conceived eventually disappeared.

Yet it is hard to see how this experience can be generalized into a recipe for universal peace. The era that ended in NATO's triumph was one in which the world was dominated by two rival and heavily armed blocs, members of both at times taking sides in civil wars in other parts of the world, and their mutual deterrence entailing big risks for their own peoples and others.

In certain circumstances a bloc, a firm military alliance against potential enemies, may seem an essential element in the defence of particular countries. But if this is to be a militarily coherent and lasting combination of fully independent states, a fairly serious and clearly defined outside threat is likely to be necessary: and the threatening power or opposing bloc is quite likely to be of broadly comparable strength. (It is perhaps significant that, though NATO still exists and has been expanding, it was far from united over 2002 and 2003.) Partial collective security on the NATO model belongs perhaps to a two-bloc world. It may at times be a necessary expedient. It is not a general solution.

A quasi-legal regime: universal collective security

This was the ideal behind the United Nations. All the existing member-states would be inviolate. There would be no allowable intervention in others' internal affairs. Aggression by any state would be resisted and reversed under the leadership of the five main victorious powers of 1945 acting together.

The principle was simple, but the necessary conditions for following it were not present. The victorious powers themselves (in each others' view) blatantly interfered in other states' internal affairs. And they were not in the smallest degree disposed to act together. At least before 1990, universal collective security under the UN never worked as intended. The Korean intervention, the only big UN military response before then, happened – as a result of two constitutional anomalies – with two of the five former allied powers on the opposing side. After 1990, when agreement among the permanent members of the Security Council was not impossible, the categories that would have allowed clear identification of states and aggressors had become confused. When were affairs internal? Were Croatia and Bosnia states attacked by Yugoslavia, or were they parts of Yugoslavia? The Kosovo action of 1999, supported by a number of the powers but not authorized by the UN Security Council, could only be justified as a humanitarian intervention (a category not recognized in the UN Charter) in what everyone agreed was legally the territory of Serbia.

What was attempted in 1945 was in fact a compromise between a legal order and a system controlled by the prevailing powers. There were rules, but the rules on matters directly related to war and peace were in effect to be interpreted by the big powers in agreement. Where the big powers failed to agree, there was a legal vacuum and other mechanisms took over. Fortunately the five permanent members could sometimes agree to authorize small-scale peacekeeping measures, which seem often to have just tipped the scales locally against fighting. So the UN was far from irrelevant to peace. And keeping the lid on small wars no doubt helped in averting large ones. It is possible also that some potential aggression was deterred by the risk, however small, that significant powers might actually have united against the aggressor. But the 1945 ideal of universal collective security as a preserver of peace was largely a dead letter between 1945 and 1990, and, except perhaps for the reversal of Iraq's invasion of Kuwait, has not shown great evidence of vitality since. Quite apart from the difficulty that the big powers would have had in agreeing, much of the fighting did not clearly meet the criteria of interstate aggression, and in the 1990s 'internal affairs' had come to seem less than sacrosanct.

This does not mean that we cannot in valuable ways develop the UN machinery and its use: by, for example, more ambitious peacekeeping and peacemaking, conciliation and arbitration instruments to take the steam out of disputes, and some attempt at clarity over the limits to humanitarian intervention. As suggested below, there are reasons for moving closer in behaviour to the norms of a legal order. Knowledge that the major powers will pay some attention to rules, at least in matters that do not closely affect their own interests, will alter the environment for others, and will tend to do so in a favourable direction. But there are likely to be limits. Where there is no consistent enforcement, supposed interests and domestic political pressures (including the pressure to do nothing) are likely to prevail over impartial interpretations of legality – and, the stronger the power, the less its calculations of interest are likely to be affected by expectations of action taken by others in defence of the rules.

Twin strategies invoking international governance

A remaining possibility, not necessarily excluding elements of the others, is to play some mix of two strategies that both involve elements of international decision- and rule-making.

One strategy is to inject as much as possible of consensual law into relations within the system of sovereign states. This is a more general expression of the United Nations ideal already mentioned. Bringing the ideal closer to fulfilment inevitably involves building on the existing multinational institutions. But there must also be changes to reflect moves in both power and sentiment since 1945. The eternal inviolability of sovereign states and the sanctity of the principle of non-intervention in internal affairs can no longer be taken as binding. (Rwanda is regularly cited as a case in which it ought not to have been followed.) As hinted above, there must probably be norms developed under which humanitarian intervention can in certain circumstances be legitimated; tribunals to deal with human-rights abuses; and conciliation and arbitration procedures over border and cultural-autonomy questions. Some of these possibilities will be broached in Chapter 5.

The approach involves not just the kind of tacit rules required by the New Realism, but explicit principles and procedures, consistent with widely held values, for settling disputes and conflicts of interest. It would aim to draw states increasingly into acceptance of the decisions of councils and tribunals over the kind of issues that might otherwise provoke insurrection and intervention. It involves a progressive extension of the area of international consensual governance – of what Ostrom (1990) calls *quasi-voluntary compliance*. However, this approach – law without an enforcer – is prone to slippage for various apparently good, or not so good, reasons. It fails to give states a reliable guarantee that, if they keep the rules, their rights will be respected.

The other strategy is to play every card for the purpose of moving toward *political organization*, political integration, ultimately across the world, and (as the most critical cases) among the West, China, Russia, and India. This would undoubtedly be a daunting task. Final success would mean a pooling of weapons and hence of remaining 'military-foreign-policy' decisions, including ultimate decisions bearing on relations among the component states. But links among groups of states need not involve this whole programme straight away. 'Widening and deepening' would both no doubt be progressive. In advance we can only speculate on the sequence in which it might happen. A variety of possible staging-posts may be supposed.

These two endeavours – at a greater intensity and scope for consensual international law and juridical institutions, and at political integration – may fortunately proceed together and indeed support each other. The former will achieve only patchy and precarious success. The latter will be gradual and slow, with no certainty of reaching its goal.

Yet this latter goal is one that gives at least some prospect of an eventual solution to the immense and horrifying challenge posed by modern warfare; it has the potential for meeting other needs of the utmost importance that are unlikely to be otherwise met; the quest for it is if anything synergistic with the drive for consensual law in the immediate future; and for these reasons it is eminently worth pursuing.

By contrast, (a) the New Realism, reviving the idea of the balance of power, probably depends, for any general success in the preservation of peace, on a measure of common values, and a degree of satisfaction with the *status quo*, among the powers, and also on some independence of policy-makers from popular emotions. (b) Long-term partial collective security among sovereign states on the NATO pattern is unlikely to play an important role without a long-term, major, and highly threatening opponent. And (c) the 'righteous-hegemony' model will leave large problems unsolved in the short and medium terms, even for the hegemon, and in the long term is unlikely to be sustainable. The more there is unchecked independence of action on the part of the hyperpower, the more inconveniently and quickly it may stimulate its nemesis, and the more it is likely to obstruct and delay a lasting solution.

What about 'unofficial' wars?

This argument has been couched in terms of the need to prevent wars between states. Yet it is of course true that much of the fighting and killing that takes place today involves unofficial forces on one or both sides. And interstate wars are often ignited by intrastate conflicts in which an outside government is drawn to the support of the unofficial, 'rebel' side. That is no reason for ignoring the importance of interstate wars. In fact it seems very likely that the path to global political organization (in a sense that excludes the possibility of independent armed states) requires the acceptance of an international (and recognizably impartial) framework of law, conciliation, and arbitration that will attend to the grievances that generate and sustain rebel movements. Without such a framework the surrender of independent armed forces will not be acceptable, and if it is not acceptable it will not happen. So a system that removes the possibility of interstate wars must necessarily be devised in such a way that it also seriously reduces the provocations that lead to wars within states.

Progressive achievement of the two must proceed hand-in-hand: peace and justice, to put it simply. Sharing the power – acceptably, which is the only way – must mean also sharing the institutions of law and the standards of judgement on a few essentials: those that concern certain human rights including cultural autonomy. Progress with each has the potential for making the other easier to attain. Fortunately the official voices of the nations agree widely in principle to a number of standards of human rights. It is turning those principles consensually into operational rules, and equipping them with accepted tribunals and recognized conciliation processes, that constitutes the challenge.

So the alleged 'new look' in warfare, new perhaps to European powers at say the beginning of the American War of Independence – the fact that much of it is not between recognized sovereign states, or at least does not start that way – does not in the least weaken the case for global political organization. It does point to a vital element in such a venture, a process that must probably move some distance among any group of potentially warring states before they agree to pool their military forces. Some flesh will be put on these assertions in later chapters.

Preventing wars is not the only reason for global political organization

Putting interstate warfare beyond the range of possibility, and making internal warfare much less likely: these are the paramount considerations, without which all else might turn out to be of little value, but they are not the only good reasons for wanting elements of world government.

There are also *environmental needs with global implications*. The most obvious at the moment is global warming. Here there is a strong case for believing that systematic action, with some immediate cost, is necessary – even if part of the case's strength lies in the uncertainty of the effects of allowing the process to continue. The action needed demands wide and disciplined co-operation among governments. Such action is not happening spontaneously, and seems unlikely to do so in the degree necessary through the political processes that we now have available. The Kyoto Protocol, which has gone closest to foreshadowing modest co-ordinated action, at least among the rich countries, provided very weak guarantees of implementation, and has now been formally abandoned by the country that is overwhelmingly the largest generator of the effect. But even if it could later be shown that the need for action on global warming was less than urgent, there is the ever-present possibility of other effects – requiring costly co-ordinated global action – that are no less serious than global warming is now widely judged to be. Ozone-layer depletion is a case that fortunately did inspire a co-ordinated response, probably because the costs of action were so puny compared with the apparent and little-disputed costs of inaction. On the other hand, we have enough experience to be able to say that preserving natural forests and the resulting biodiversity, or relatively clean oceans, will not be so easily accomplished. And there might be other threats, such as an encounter with a large meteor, which the technology of the time might make it possible to avert, but only at the cost of considerable diversion and concentration of resources.

Moreover, if we fail to avert the damage due to environmental changes, we may then need co-ordinated action in order to deal with their ill-effects. For example, if and when global warming should lead to risks of repeated or permanent flooding of low-lying coastal areas, in some of which there are huge numbers of people, mainly poor, the world may find itself with the choice of either building very expensive sea-walls and flood-control systems or resettling people in their millions. It may have to do both. Either would be fiendishly costly, and the second also a political minefield. Even if both turned out to be technically possible, it is hard to see either as eventuating without a world authority that has powers of taxation. And the effects of failure to do either or both are too terrible to contemplate. As another example, failure of states and their peoples to take action for conserving water may well aggravate disputes over rivers that readily come to be seen as matters of life and death. An impartial power that can impose a settlement and possibly mitigate the resulting grievances of both parties may be the salvation of both.

There is also a strong case for saying that a measure of world authority is needed *to check abuses of the most basic human rights* and *to remedy those elements of extreme poverty that in a technical sense can easily be mended.* For the inhabitants of those countries that are affluent and in which civil rights are largely protected, the ground for concern about these matters is the human sympathy and solidarity and mutual respect that are both commonly felt and also generally recognized as among the essential manifestations of human dignity. We should and we do care about the sufferings and abuses of our fellows, at least when there is a possibility, however slight, of mitigating them. If we do not, or pretend that we do not, we deface or malign our distinctively human character.

We do not, and should not, rest easy while people anywhere are enslaved, or tortured and raped and killed with the sanction of the authorities, or imprisoned unjustly or unnecessarily, or punished for expressing certain views or speaking certain languages. There is every reason to believe that these abuses will continue to occur unless and until the authorities in every country recognize a common code, and a common system for its last-resort enforcement. That implies a final authority superior to every purely national authority.

There is also the question of extreme poverty and social injustice. How the world fails to deal now with the most rudimentary demands of material welfare was starkly illustrated at the start of 2003 by the position as it was then understood in much of Southern and Eastern Africa. Starvation early in 2003 was said to threaten 30 million people. At the same time, HIV/AIDS affected huge numbers: in the worst-affected countries (on end-1999 figures) at up to 25 per cent, even 36 per cent, of their adult populations (Lowenson and Whiteside 2001: 3), with incidence in many cases still rising, medical services mostly far too stretched to give adequate care, and in most countries no widespread provision of the expensive medicines which alone can delay and mitigate the symptoms. AIDS has greatly boosted the incidence of tuberculosis, and worldwide there were expected by 2010 to have been 40 million more orphaned children than would have existed in its absence (ibid.: 5).

In the face of such disasters, the World Food Program, with its limited funding, and national food contributions, have together often proved seriously inadequate to meet food deficits. And a fund set up on the appeal of the Secretary-General of the United Nations for $7–10 billion a year (around 0.03 per cent, that is 3/10,000, of world income) to fight AIDS, tuberculosis, and malaria seemed likely at the end of 2002 to be financed to the extent of only $2 billion in its first year. Much fragmented and half-hearted goodwill is not enough to see that these absolutely basic needs – requiring tiny fractions of world income – are met. Only an authority with taxing powers, responsible in the last resort for reacting to the extremes of need across the world – because it is responsible to the people of the world in rough proportion to their numbers – is likely to prove adequate to satisfy the most sparing demands of social justice and human compassion. The fact that the governments of some of the countries seriously affected have acted with gross irresponsibility, or worse, in these matters is far from being a counter-argument. As with civil rights, citizens in an international confederation might well have judicial or other remedies against certain extremes of economic and social abuse on the part of their states' governments.

War and peace, cross-border environmental destruction and its aftermath, human rights, extremes of avoidable poverty: these – probably these alone – are the subjects for which a world authority, with taxing powers and a legal monopoly of military force, are necessary. How an authority meeting these conditions might be made acceptable (and therefore how it might – eventually – be attained with general consent); how we might gain a reasonable assurance that the cure will not prove worse than the disease; what constitutional devices might work; why certain other subjects involving important global public-goods are not included; by what process the goal might be reached: these, closely interlocked, questions will be considered in later chapters.

Is it possible?

States have never voluntarily amalgamated

This is of course not true. The least questionable examples include Switzerland, the Netherlands, the USA, Canada, Australia. In each case, it was a decision from within the communities that joined together and as popular as existing forms of government allowed. Significantly the unions in these cases were all confederations or federations, or both in succession, not unitary states.

Conversion of the kingdoms of Scotland and England first into a dynastic union and then into a unitary state could be argued either way. But the unifications of Garibaldi's Italy and Bismarck's Germany – unwelcome as they may have been in the ruling circles of Naples and Rome and Munich and the rest – were probably on balance popular. Bismarck made his own use of a popular national and liberal movement which, left to itself, might have opted for an even larger Germany.

Those that have voluntarily joined have had close cultural and historical affinities

On the face of it, this is true of all those cases just cited, with the arguable exception of Canada. (I ignore the many instances of peoples unified politically as an imperialist legacy, as in South Asia, Africa, Indonesia, the Philippines.)

Yet the European Union shows signs of breaking the rule. It is not a federation. Nor does it yet correspond to the usual image of a confederation, which has normally involved at least a union of all members for defence. But it is a union for a number of important purposes, for some of which the member-states have no individual licence to block joint decisions. Most of its members, covering a big majority of its population, are members of NATO, a defence union with its own command structure that is probably not much different in constitutional form from some of the defence unions that have counted as confederations in the past.

Certainly the peoples of the EU have lived close together on a fairly small fraction of the world's land. Certainly all of them, including those due to enter in 2004, have shared a predominantly Christian tradition for many centuries. Culturally all have drawn on Israel, Greece, and Rome, partly through Arab intermediaries; and for several centuries there has been much cultural interchange among them.

Yet the member-states of the Union include the successors of five of those six European Great Powers of the early twentieth century whose disputes and hostilities were almost entirely responsible for ignition of the two world wars of that century's first half. It was designed as a union of enemies – in the hope of tying them together so that further war should be impossible. And this mission is being pursued further with the inclusion in 2004 of at least seven states whose peoples were formally deadly enemies of most of the rest through much of the previous half-century.

It is easy to sneer at this as trivial because it has happened. But, viewed from 1939 or even 1945, any idea of incorporating the first twelve members – or, viewed from as late as 1985, of adding the next thirteen – would have seemed highly optimistic, if not utopian.

Moreover, the possibility of Turkey's entry has been affirmed on both sides – a large population of Muslim tradition, at present significantly poorer than most of the twenty-five that form the union from 2004. Cultural and historical affinities do not immediately spring to mind when one thinks of Turkey and Ireland or Turkey and Sweden.

Europeans are peculiar and the rest of the world has other instincts

A further argument, now sometimes heard from American commentators, is that the propensity to join together is a special quirk of Europeans, a peculiarity of European culture and outlook. Other people, it is said, think differently. But sixty years ago the idea that the Germans and the French were just waiting to throw in their lot together would have seemed bizarre – as strange as the view that the same was true of Pakistanis and Indians, or of Koreans and Japanese, would seem now. It was presumably some combination of bitter experience in the meantime, new threats faced in common, and imaginative leadership, that made the difference. And, for at least some of those that have joined the Union, the hope of material benefits appears to have played a part. The choice of potential postulants over whether or not they will seek or accept entry has largely been debated in economic terms.

What Robert Cooper (1996) calls the post-modern state – distinguished by the recent tendency of governments, especially in Europe, to submit their actions to mutual scrutiny and restraint – has not strikingly been a longstanding European propensity. It is much easier to see moves in that direction as motivated by rationally considered choices. Cooper sees 'post-modern Europe' as beginning with the Treaty of Rome and the Treaty on Conventional Forces in Europe: the former 'created out of the failures of the modern system: the balance-of-power that ceased to work and the nation state which took nationalism to destructive extremes'; the latter 'born of the failures, wastes and absurdities of the Cold War' (ibid.: 22–3). 'The modern European strategic culture', says Robert Kagan (2002: 4), in an essay not unreservedly enthusiastic about what he sees as current European attitudes, 'is a conscious rejection of the European past, of machtpolitik'.

States with high rule-of-law and human-rights standards will not join those with low standards

This is true enough. Any union in which the Western democracies (for all their faults) are prepared to join will inevitably impose the sort of requirements for membership that the European Union formally demands now: democracy, the rule of law, respect for human rights, in particular those of minorities.

But if membership of a union has recognized advantages to offer, these entry conditions can very well act as a spur to potential members for improved performance. At the moment it seems that the carrot of membership has been influencing practice and sentiment in Turkey and Turkish Cyprus, and influencing it in a big way. Observance of these norms is not an all-or-nothing matter. They have emerged gradually, and the reasonably good performers still have failures. Countries that are some part of the way to an acceptable level of observance may be edged further along. If there are rewards for maintaining certain standards, those standards will be encouraged. As the Economist (18.1.2003: 41) put it in connection with pressure for the unification of Cyprus: 'EU officials sometimes lament that the Union has only one cudgel in its diplomatic bag: the offer of membership. Maybe. But it is one hell of a cudgel.'

Moreover, joining a union that maintains these standards is likely to have a ratchet effect on their observance by the joiner. Though most of the European human-rights machinery formally covers all members of the Council of Europe, membership of the EU provides additional pressure for taking its requirements and its institutions seriously. And, once conforming, they are unlikely in the new environment to turn back.

To repeat: incorporating all or most of the world in a democratic confederation is not likely to happen suddenly or soon. But the very business of overcoming the obstacles that it faces will be a salutary one. The conditions and rewards of entry have the potential for improving precisely those practices that now form one of the main blocks in the way.

Rich populations cannot be expected to join in democratic unions with poor populations . . .

The history of EU enlargement shows that this is over-simple. In the 1980s the Union admitted Greece, Spain, and Portugal (as earlier Ireland) though they were significantly poorer than the existing members and would on balance be subsidized. In 2004 it has admitted ten more applicants, all distinctly poorer than the average. They too will be subsidized. Clearly there are other considerations than whether the new can expect to represent a fiscal charge on the old.

. . . at least if the poor populations are much more numerous

There is a serious point here. What if, in a democratic union with powers of taxation, the numerous poor were to gang up on the much-less-numerous rich and to engineer a big redistribution of income? Surely that possibility would deter the rich nations from ever joining such a confederation with that balance of numbers. At the moment those people earning less than average world income vastly outnumber those earning more. The disparity, however income comparisons are made, is extreme. Moreover, as is the way with income-distributions, this excess of the below-average numbers over the above-average (a so-called positively skewed distribution) is always likely to be with us, even if not in such an acute form as now. Surely this makes a global association with the normal characteristics of a democratic government out of the question.

The first point that might be made against this proposition is that exactly the same fear of the effects of democracy (that it would lead inevitably to plunder of the upper and even the middle classes, to dispossession of the few by the many, and to a levelling of income that would remove all incentives) was long held among the more privileged within individual nations. As democracy along one-person-one-vote lines was gingerly approached, it became clear that the fears were exaggerated. Though fully fledged democracy did lead to some equalizing redistribution, it was very far in most countries from obliterating the rich and the middle classes or overthrowing the institutions of property. Indeed it was only in certain totalitarian states that private property was to any substantial degree eliminated. Most of the time democracy has been pretty lenient on the rich.

True, this experience will not necessarily be repeated when it is a matter of poor and rich nations, with vast differences between their average incomes. And members of the rich nations – including their poor, privileged by world standards – may not be prepared to take the risk.

However, this, it may be argued, merely points to the need for certain constitutional safeguards if a democratic confederation is to be acceptable. Briefly, there must be blocking powers that the representatives of certain countries, if they are sufficiently united, can in the last resort use against new fiscal measures. The powers need not be given in any asymmetric pattern to the representatives of rich nations exclusively or preferentially. (A way of achieving this will be explained in Chapter 6.) They need not, and almost certainly will not, preclude some equalizing redistribution. They will merely provide a safeguard against measures that overwhelming sentiment in the rich countries (or in any comparable group of countries) considers excessive.

Safeguards such as these are probably part of the price for the chance to form a democratic confederation covering much of the world – so long as that world has an income distribution between nations such as the one that holds today. But I shall try to show that safeguards can be devised that will convince the richer populations that they need not submit to an income redistribution that they would find intolerable.

The greatest obstacle

There are, of course, huge obstacles to effective democratic political organization covering the world: to a union that enables the world to act in certain critical respects as one.

But the greatest obstacle is that no one is discussing it. Such a union is not now widely regarded, among the people of the world – that is among those whose opinions count politically – as an objective that ought to be actively sought. And surely one highly important reason is that a union of that kind is not thought possible. At least there is no prevailing plausible vision of what it might be like and of the means by which it might be attained.

What I try to do here is to give a picture of both the position at which we might aim and the road for reaching it. The picture has a chance of being plausible provided that it appears generally tolerable – provided, that is, that it appears unlikely to deprive any group of people (other than certain very limited elites that happen to be holding power, mostly in ill-governed states, and often precariously) of what they value – while at the same time it brings large and widely dispersed dividends.

To show that there is both a goal and a path that meets these tests is the main purpose of this book.

Summary of Chapter 2

- There is abundant evidence of the dangers of a world of independently armed states, especially given the existence of nuclear weapons and other weapons of mass destruction.

- Any hope in the post-Cold-War world that a single righteous, overwhelmingly powerful hyperpower may set all right by acting on its own judgement as the world's policeman is unpromising, even from the standpoint of those that form the constituency of the hyperpower and of those that believe in its righteousness.

- The prospect of maintaining peace through a balance of power – that is by tacit rules aimed at preventing any government or alliance of governments from becoming markedly stronger than its potential competitors – is also not good given the difficulties in the past of forming such systems, their fragility once formed, and the manifest absence today of the necessary conditions for their maintenance.

- Partial collective-security, as effected under NATO during the Cold War, probably depends on the existence of a single, uniquely threatening enemy and is therefore not generalizable. That example also illustrates the dangers that may attend it.

- Universal collective-security, as projected by the founders of the UN, would depend on conditions that have not existed in the meantime: certainly not before 1990 and very imperfectly after.

- We cannot exclude the use of elements of these approaches. Failing complete security from any of them, however, we are left, in the search for a long-term peace-preserving strategy, with a choice of some mix between (a) pursuing a workable regime of consensual international law that builds further on the formal and actual UN structure, stemming from 1945, in ways that reflect current sentiment and experience in the meantime, and (b) seeking a path to political integration among the potentially competing powers. Success in the former of these ventures is likely to prove unreliable; the goal of the latter is uncertain of attainment and can be reached at best only gradually. But the attempts are mutually consistent; and indeed one may support the other and compensate for its failings.

- Unofficial wars form a large part of current warfare and are frequently the occasion of such official wars as there are; but political integration of a governmental kind, through instruments for dealing with complaints of group injustice, has the potential for reducing the occasion for unofficial wars.

- Beside preventing wars, political integration is likely to be necessary for averting some major cross-border environmental threats or alternatively for dealing with their human ill-effects; for establishing universal respect for basic civil and political rights; and for fulfilling the most rudimentary requirements of world social justice by concerted movement toward setting a floor to poverty.

- A number of popular arguments against the possibility of any form or degree of world government are shown to be faulty in the generalizations of fact on which they rely.

- But the biggest obstacle facing any approach to global political integration remains the fact that there is no strong movement in its favour. And this is mainly because it is generally not thought possible; there is no plausible vision of what it might be like and how it could be achieved.

- This book aims to help fill that gap in vision.

Note

1. This account draws on recollected broadcasts of the 'Kennedy tapes' with recent comment by Robert McNamara and others; on *Keesing's Record of World Events*; and on 'At daggers drawn' by Philip Knightley and Peter Pringle, *The Independent*, 6.10.1992: 19.

Chapter 3

Forms of global association available

The idea of a world government, on the same lines as national governments, looks at first glance both frightening and politically out of the question. Even the idea of a world federation seems far from the agenda, if a federation means something comparable in constitution to the United States of America or India or Germany or Australia, in which the armed forces, and many other central functions of government, are controlled exclusively, or at least with overriding power, from the centre, and there is no constitutional procedure by which any of the components can withdraw.

However, there is a range of other devices, well short of a federation along North American lines, by which groups of states have arranged to act in concert. Some of these have been used, mainly since the Second World War, as co-ordinating mechanisms for the world as a whole.

What has been called 'the economic theory of the state' has run along somewhat the following lines. There are a number of goods that people generally want or need but that will not be adequately provided so long as everyone acts independently in her or his own interests: policing, administration of the law, support for the destitute, public protection against infectious diseases, pure water, a guaranteed measure of health and education services for all. The term *public-good* is applied in a narrow sense to some of these benefits, and in a broad sense to all of them and more. The uncoordinated pursuit of individual interest is inadequate to provide these goods, and for some of them the necessary co-ordination would require individual restraint or sacrifice which not all would be willing to accept unless compelled under sanctions to do so. So, it is argued, a superior coercive power – a government – is needed, at least to deal with this latter category. On similar reasoning, it can be argued that, because there are highly important world-public-goods which the uncoordinated action of individual states pursuing their independent 'national' interests will not secure, and over which the observance of voluntary agreements will be difficult to guarantee, we need at least a degree of world government.

Yet it is not only through the coercive power of the state that individuals combine for common purposes. Neighbours may agree to contribute time or money to create a public park or to protect each other from crime. People form clubs for a great variety of purposes and agree to abide by the rules so long as they remain members. Some purely voluntary associations have a military discipline, which their members accept, even though no one compels them to do so. Even in relation to that much-discussed function of the state, prevention of the over-exploitation of common resources, Ostrom (1990) has catalogued a number of cases, from widely dispersed parts of the earth, in which communities have limited their members' access to common pastures or water supplies through rules that have been successfully followed, entirely without coercion, and in some cases for centuries.

Consensual unions and governmental unions

In the same way states have combined, more or less closely, for common purposes, without giving any higher power the irrevocable licence to coerce them. I shall divide the forms in which they have done this into *agencies*, *conventions*, *clubs*, *voluntary tribunals*, *quasi-confederations*, and *confederations* – all of them short of the 1787-type North American *federation*. The first four will be called *consensual unions*; the other two, together with full federations, *governmental unions*. The dividing-line between consensual and governmental is not always clear, and the terms do not precisely nail the distinction, which is really based on a combination of several criteria, but the division and subdivisions are worth making to illustrate the variety of possibilities.

Agencies are ventures into which states commit resources but otherwise do not bind themselves to engage in, or to refrain from, particular courses of action. Probably the World Bank, the IMF since 1971, and *de facto*, some might judge, the United Nations complex as a whole, come into this category: organizations without rules binding on the members except that they should contribute resources according to some schedule.

Conventions on their own are rules without organizations. The rules are usually negative and broad, binding the members to refrain from some activity: chemical warfare, landmine-laying. But some, such as START, the CFE treaty, and other arms-limitation treaties concluded around the end of the Cold War, have had precise and complex positive provisions about such matters as withdrawal, destruction, and monitoring. Though there may be no specific organization, there may be well-specified procedures in these cases, such as for mutual inspection.

Clubs will be taken to indicate combinations in which there are both rules and an organization, but covering a specific limited field of activity: cases such as the World Trade Organization (and GATT); the IMF before 1971 (with its rules on exchange-rates); and the Council of Europe (with its human-rights regime). Clubs will necessarily have some institution for determining whether or not the rules are being observed and hence of interpreting those rules in doubtful cases. There may be sanctions against breaking the rules, and the ultimate sanction is expulsion from the organization with consequent loss of the benefits of membership. But strictly there is no coercion. Compliance is quasi-voluntary in the sense used by Ostrom (1990).

Voluntary tribunals may be regarded as a subset of clubs. They cover instances such as the International Criminal Court or the European Court of Human Rights. Those states that accept either of these institutions will treat it as if it were a court of law. But no one compels them to accept it. Moral and diplomatic pressures, or the desire to encourage the participation of others, supported more or less by a sense that acceptance is *right*, or the fact that there are tangible rewards for doing so, persuade states to adhere.

Agencies, conventions, clubs, and voluntary tribunals can be covered by the term *consensual unions*. (The class can be extended if we incude what can broadly be called *networks*: associations that involve in their participation or direction representatives other than those of state governments. They may otherwise have the nature of agencies or clubs or else simply forums for discussion.) Each has a strictly limited scope of activity, and broadly it can be said that any expansion of at least their *areas* of rule-making and of the corresponding obligations imposed on members must be decided consensually among the member-governments. Further, it can probably be said that all their policy decisions are made, unanimously or not, by member-governments. Any executive officers that such a union has (separate from the spokespersons of the constituting governments) are essentially civil servants whose rulings have the function of interpreting agreed rules and policies within the limited area that the particular union covers.

It goes without saying that states that join these unions may withdraw from them.

But then there are associations that have more of the characteristics of government. These will be labelled quasi-confederations, true confederations, and federations, and will be classed together as *governmental unions*.

Quasi-confederations will be taken to include institutions such as the European Union which, beyond the features of a club, have some of the usual constitutional forms of a government, reflecting the fact that they have an executive function (involving some fairly wide discretion) rather than simply one of interpreting and developing a convention or rules and policies laid down by member-governments; that they cover a range of different spheres for their decision-making; and that they have a legislative function, for making new rules, or even for extending their rule-making into new areas, that at least does not *necessarily* depend entirely on the consensus, or even necessarily on any form of majority decision, of member-governments. Yet the *quasi-* prefix is taken to mean that they do not dispose of the armed forces of their members or have superior armed forces of their own. Calling them confederations implies here that (*de facto* at least) they do allow their members freely to withdraw.

True confederations, as I shall use the term, differ from quasi-confederations in the one vital point that they dispose of armed forces, including most or all of the military forces of their members. (As a result, almost inevitably, they have an overriding role in a number of aspects of foreign policy.) The archetypal historical confederations (the Swiss Cantons from the thirteenth century, the Netherlands cities from the sixteenth, the North American States between 1781 and 1788) have in fact been formed mainly for this purpose: for the sake of common defence or the prosecution of a war. Fighting a war demanded that there should at least be a military commander who had considerable executive discretion. Members of true confederations, as the term is used here, still have a right to withdraw.

We do not specify in these definitions whether confederations (quasi- or true) have a power of imposing taxes independently of the specific agreement of the governments or legislatures of all of their member-states. Most of the historical confederations have not initially possessed this power. The EU today has powers of taxation under its own constitutional procedures, but any extension of the *sources* of revenue would require consensus among member-governments.

The dividing-line between *federations* and *confederations* in common usage is unclear. For present purposes, I shall treat it as hanging on one simple point: whether it is generally recognized and accepted that any of the component states has a right, entirely on its own decision, to secede. This need not be actually stated; the constitutional documents may even appear to deny it; but, so long as it is undoubtedly true in fact, what is present is not a federation. Canada still appears to be a federation on this test. There is no explicit mention of secession in its 1982 Constitution. Though Quebec will very probably be allowed to secede in certain conditions, it seems that any decision on whether or not it may do so, and under what conditions, will, as an act of government, be made by Canada and Quebec jointly, not by Quebec on its own. By contrast, no one doubts that, if Sweden or Denmark chose, in a decision made under its own constitutional processes, to leave the European Union, it would simply do so, without the need to seek anyone else's permission, regardless of what the other members of the Union thought and regardless of the wording of any treaties. (The draft Union Constitution presented in June 2004 would make this right explicit.)

A *federation*, as the term has generally been understood in the past two centuries, would have taxing powers independently of its member-governments (as a confederation might or might not), though the forms of tax that it was permitted to collect might be constitutionally limited; would control the significant armed forces within its borders; and would have an overriding role in all aspects of foreign policy. In practice, federations in the twentieth century have controlled much else – currency, monetary policy, posts, foreign trade – but these functions may be considered detachable. In addition, we are using the term to imply that the members may not, according to the rules accepted in practice, unilaterally withdraw. This question was settled *de facto* for the United States of America in 1861–5.

Agencies, conventions, clubs, and voluntary tribunals do not bind a state to any action or any limitation on its own decisions except in particular limited areas of activity within which it has explicitly agreed that the union may bind it while it remains a member. Its government will have consented to the limited fields of rule-making under which it may be bound, if not to every specific rule individually. A confederation *may* bind it with a wider range of discretion (the member-state may have agreed to a constitution that enables its own choices to be overridden in certain major matters, not only of specific rules but also of the areas of rule-making covered, or of executive action that goes beyond the interpretation of agreed rules), but the member still has the expedient in the last resort of unbinding itself by leaving the union. So, in spite of the usefulness of this consensual–governmental division, confederations – like agencies, conventions, clubs, and voluntary tribunals – may still be regarded as examples of 'quasi-voluntary compliance'. Withdrawal, however, will have costs, generally more so from a confederation than from a more limited association, and a government or people is unlikely to have joined unless it has had at the time a reasonable confidence in the constitutional processes of the union and the likely intentions of its fellow-members. A federation will of course have required an even greater degree of confidence.

There are no doubt borderline cases between consensual and governmental unions as defined here. The United Nations, through the Security Council, may in certain circumstances behave ostensibly like a confederation, and do so (arguably at least) in accordance with its Charter. It may take military action that some of the members of the Security Council, or other members of the UN, oppose, and take it under rules whose interpretation necessitates wide discretion. Yet common parlance would certainly not call the UN a confederation. *De facto* there are large differences of degree between the UN as an organization and the weakest of the associations that would normally be given that epithet.

In order to make the world in the necessary respects autonomous – able to act for its people as an entity – it seems *prima facie* reasonable to take the least controversial forms of association – agencies, conventions, clubs, and voluntary tribunals – as far as they will go, with no resort to a governmental-type union (quasi- or true confederation, or federation) unless the purposes intended cannot be served without it. And, if that further step does have to be taken, the next reasonable goal is a confederation – with the escape-hatch quite explicitly marked – rather than a federation.

So, sorting out a practical vision for an autonomous world – one that can deal with global public-goods in the broadest sense, namely global common purposes in general – requires us to make judgements over which further necessary functions are suited to agencies, conventions, clubs, or voluntary tribunals; and which require quasi- or true confederations. And, if there are some in the latter class, we need to see how the confederations may be made sufficiently attractive, and have sufficient safeguards, that governments and peoples may be willing to join them and to remain within them.

What are the functions that need to be performed jointly for the world as a whole (because independent action by individuals and governments is unlikely to meet the needs) but are not adequately covered by existing institutions? Briefly these are (a) a number of aspects of economic stabilization, which has long been, but is if anything increasingly, a global problem; (b) maintaining the capacity of governments and international organizations to collect revenue fairly and consistently, in the face of competitive forces and internationally open financial institutions that are likely to render it difficult; (c) a substantially open international-trade regime; (d) making the necessary redistribution of resources to support and stimulate anti-poverty programmes (for health, education, accessible water, for example, as well as general income) in order to satisfy the most rudimentary requirements of world social justice; (e) securing joint action against environmental threats of global character; (f) upholding basic human rights; and, last but far from least, (g) keeping the peace.

For some of these purposes, consensual unions are all that is needed. For others, consensual unions may have to be pressed into action first, but if so with the aim of progressing to governmental unions in order that the necessary functions may be adequately served. What sort of union we need for each of these seven purposes?

Unions: consensual or governmental

Economic stabilization

World action for economic stabilization is of enormous importance. Much of the complaint against 'globalization' rests on the instability that it is held to generate. But, for clear reasons, the international measures for stabilization that are necessary and possible can plausibly be provided, and are probably best provided, by *agencies*. In fact the IMF, the agency already concerned with economic stabilization, might well have its functions extended to do much of the rest of what is required. There are several big remaining jobs to be done.

These involve transferring to the global or interstate field devices that are commonplaces within national economic management or private commerce or both. The devices are compensatory finance, bankruptcy, and insurance.

These three functions, by no means excluding other forms of co-operation for stabilization, are quite consistent with maintaining the international bodies managing them as merely agencies. The reason why this has good prospects of being feasible politically is that rules of action can readily be constructed so that their operation, given reasonable technical competence, is likely to benefit virtually everyone involved, certainly the peoples of all or nearly all states considered as entities. Rationality and imagination in the elaboration of the agencies' briefs and structures are the only other qualities demanded. No nation or significant body of people need be required to make tangible sacrifices. The obstacles are in the fields of ideology, stereotyped thinking, and institutional inertia: formidable perhaps, but potentially subject to rational attack.

At the same time, measures in these areas, in particular the management of macroeconomic stabilization, can be highly sensitive politically. So there are important potential advantages in leaving unfettered power over this function in national hands, with international measures simply aiming to fill the gaps. Not only is a consensual global association potentially adequate for the co-ordination needed. Aspiring to go further and to work with a governmental union may well be counter-productive. Trying to run a single macroeconomic regime, rather than simply seeking to fill the gaps left internationally by national regimes, risks making the global authority highly vulnerable to critical attack. Moreover, there are intrinsic difficulties of stabilizing through a single international macroeconomic regime. Its controls are likely to be too crude. At any particular time, what is the right monetary policy for one national economy may well work in precisely the wrong direction for another. Centralizing the controls over divergent economies may well therefore be destabilizing rather than the reverse. (Arguably these difficulties have already appeared in the attempt at a single system of monetary control, with crude fiscal limits, for most of the members of the European Union. Monetary policies that have been too 'tight' for Germany have been too 'lax' for Ireland and the Netherlands. The fiscal limits have seemed so inappropriate for economies at times when they lack adequate effective demand that they have been widely disregarded.) An authority attempting such central control could well be justifiably unpopular because its brief could not of its nature be satisfactorily fulfilled.

Maintaining state revenues in the face of globalization

Maintaining government revenue, in the face of the cross-border mobility of capital and enterprise (complicated by corruption and international crime), also has the potential for being dealt with by a consensual union – in this case most effectively, it seems, by a *club*, involving both a convention and an organization. There is no need for uniformity in the taxes imposed by various countries, let alone for an international organization to play any role in actual tax administration. Beside the scope that capital mobility gives to tax evasion when tax systems have been designed without international co-operation, certain elements of 'competition' between tax jurisdictions in their quest to attract inward investment, and of executive discretion within them, have a tendency to deplete the sources of revenue; and there need to be conventions and pacts to limit both practices. There are a number of detailed ways in which the leakage of revenue legally due can be avoided, and some of these require appropriate rules to be observed by tax authorities and some exchange of information among them. In the attack on tax evasion and other criminal activity, certain information requirements need also to be imposed jointly on banks. None of this need impinge on the deliberate social choices that particular countries make about their tax rates, but it is likely to take considerable negotiation, for which a champion and a forum will be extremely valuable. Hence the arguable need for an interstate organization on somewhat similar lines to the World Trade Organization: a standing forum, with dedicated expert staff, to foster negotiation of mutually beneficial deals that can acceptably be generalized.[1]

It is always likely that some small territories at least will see advantage for themselves in remaining as tax havens and refuse to join the club. This might superficially suggest the advantage of a *governmental union*, in which in which rules for all could be legislated and the minority of states would have to yield to the majority. But for the present purpose this is an illusion. We take it as a premiss that any union will have to be formed by consent. A proposed union that was to have prevailing powers over the tax system might well be unacceptable not only to the existing small tax-haven states but also to major countries that might nonetheless be fully prepared to co-operate in consensual unions. Moreover, once the preponderant economic weight of the world is within such clubs, it may well be possible to limit the damage done by those holding out, possibly even to compensate them for losses.

The reason why mending the international leaks in tax systems has good prospects of success through consensual methods is similar to the one given over economic stabilization. At least all the big national players – the governments of countries of significant size, rich and poor – have gains to be made, and the interests within their domains who would suffer, if not actually criminals, are at least people who have used, or recommended, or profited from, ways of frustrating the lawful intentions of public authorities. Admittedly some of the countries that are small players have flourished, or at least supported themselves, by providing channels of evasion and avoidance against the taxes of other countries. Admittedly too there may be personal conflicts of interest on the part of powerful individuals in politics and administration that can mitigate their zeal for improving the collection of revenue. However, the fact remains that the large bulk of the world's population, rich and poor, live in states whose revenue, and quite arguably their peoples' welfare, stands to gain clearly and speedily from international co-operation. Any gains from free-riding on the part of a few members can fairly readily be nullified by the majority. In fact, negotiation (which has already begun) among the bulk of the OECD countries on common action may achieve much of the purpose of the endeavour and give impetus to the rest.

On the other hand, as with economic stabilization, subjecting tax structure to a single international control is not only extremely unlikely to be accepted but also likely, if it were adopted, to be a potent source of friction.

An open-trade regime

Whatever qualifications have to be made, there are clearly large advantages that flow from a substantially free system of international trade. The obstacles to it have been nationalist-protectionist ideologies, fortified by particular industrial interests and by the genuine doubt that may exist about the welfare balance of particular measures of liberalization at the specific times they are considered. There is always likely too to be a conflict between the general long-term material advantage (to all countries, if not to all individuals and localities) of freeing trade, and on the other hand the short-term disruption and destruction, and perhaps longer-term cultural homogenization and adverse environmental effects, that may appear to be attached to particular instances of it. As a result much of the action taken toward freeing (visible and invisible) trade and other international transactions is highly controversial.

In joining together in the World Trade Organization (WTO), most of the governments of the world have committed themselves on balance to freer trade, whatever their reservations. The processes of GATT and the WTO since the Second World War have led to considerable reduction of barriers, though the net effect is widely regarded as unbalanced between the interests of industrialized and those of developing countries. Barriers maintained by rich countries to imports (or their subsidization of exports) of foodstuffs and labour-intensive manufactures have been specially persistent. By contrast, pressure has controversially been put on developing countries in recent years for openness to financial services and for rigorous observance of certain types of patent.

The question here is whether the genuine advantages of freer world trade are likely to be better achieved – and with less adverse side-effects – as a result of an attempt to set up a 'governmental' world trade authority than with the existing club-type arrangement. (Formally, the WTO proceeds through consensus, though inevitably some members carry much more weight informally than others.) Awkwardly in some ways for the main theme of this book, I would answer no. As with macroeconomic stabilization, trade policy is highly controversial, and the reasons for resisting or modifying liberalization, good and bad, are specific to individual countries. Liberalization centrally imposed, rather than consensually negotiated, risks excessive aggravation. (The European Union has managed a single trade policy, but at the cost of accepting agricultural arrangements that represent a costly and destructive homage to a few rich farmers, a penalty on a number of poor countries, and a considerable obstacle to Union enlargement. However, there is now good reason for thinking that the elements of the policy that are most damaging, to the people of the Union and to those outside, will be progressively abandoned; and each new accession is likely to favour reform.)

An attempt to lay down a world trade policy from the centre is likely to be political dynamite. By contrast, the slow, consensual processes taking place under the wings of GATT and the WTO have made considerable progress. Their main faults are due to the imbalance of bargaining power, which may in part be remediable.

Financing the attack on extreme poverty

The very sanguine may hope that consensual arrangements among nations (such as rich–poor bargains in which development aid under whatever guise is traded for concessions of particular concern to the rich, such as elements of environmental protection), plus appropriate intermediation as through commercialized microfinance, plus the relevant elements of free trade and free markets, plus community mobilization, plus the action of governments in low-income and middle-income countries supplemented by voluntary aid from the rich, will go some way to overcoming the extremes of world poverty. But the redistribution of public resources across states that appears to be required – for any serious approach to what we might regard as the most elemental level of world social justice to be realized within one or two decades – seems to be such that rich countries, operating independently by their internal constitutional processes, are unlikely to release enough funds for the purpose.

It is not that a really large proportion of their annual income would be needed. On World Bank figures for 1998, a transfer of $226 billion a year, only 1 per cent of the GNP of the high-income countries (a little higher as a proportion than the 0.9 per cent stated as necessary annually for development and environment purposes for the succeeding eight years by the Rio Conference of June 1992), would represent 12.3 per cent of the GNP of low-income countries, or 6.6 per cent of the GNP of low-income and lower-middle-income countries taken together. (In these comparisons exchange-rate-equivalents are used, as probably more relevant for the present purpose than PPP equivalents.)

Properly allocated this could form an enormous boost to the whole range of infrastructure, health, education, environment, and general anti-poverty programmes in those countries. But it would be about four times as high as the annual amount currently transferred to the Third World in Official Development Assistance; much higher than the overall proportion of rich-country annual income *ever* so transferred in the past fifty years of such aid; and nearly half as high again as the proportion (0.7 per cent) taken as a standing target by the United Nations. Yet 1 per cent of GNP is well below the annual real increment of GNP in most affluent countries (many with virtually static populations) in most years. It could hardly be said to represent any striking sacrifice. There is a big gap between on the one hand modest estimates of what could and should be done by the world community toward health, education, water, sanitation and other basic welfare objectives in the interests of social justice, and on the other hand what seems likely to be done under present institutions.[2]

So, though there should be no neglect of the need for action now through the machinery presently available, experience points to the need for a governmental union in which the political forum deciding how much will be devoted to combating the poverty of poor countries should be one that represents the people of those countries themselves as well as those of the rich – and with power in some degree related to their relative populations.

But could the member-nations of the affluent world ever consent to join such a union in which others, much poorer than themselves, would have a say over how *their* (the rich countries') own wealth was to be used? Possibly so, but only under two conditions. One is that there should be fairly substantial benefits to the rich countries – or specific and visible changes valued by large and articulate sections of their populations – expected from such a union. The other is that, within the union, the rich countries together should in the last resort have a veto over its revenue and spending. To elaborate on a point made in Chapter 2, this latter condition suggests the need for a particular form of constitution for the union: one in which, for certain purposes including money bills, the representatives of the member-nations should vote as a certain number of 'houses' (representing regional or other interest groups) with each house able to exercise a veto over any change. One of the houses might be constituted by the representatives of the rich countries, or one each by North America and Europe. In the latter case, each of the two could set a limit on the extent that the rich could be soaked. (How this might work is further discussed in Chapter 6.)

At first glance it might seem that this would leave anti-poverty redistribution no further forward than it would have been if each rich country was still making its own decisions about how much to contribute. But to conclude this would be to ignore how politics is likely to work in a governmental union, at least in one in which the power is predominantly in the hands of representatives directly and proportionately elected for the purpose rather than in the gift of member-governments. If we suppose a broadly British-type democratic model – of an executive responsible to a parliament elected in rough proportion to population numbers – poor-country representatives would greatly outnumber those of rich countries. The executive would need considerable support among poor-country representatives. To gain power and pursue their objectives, representatives and factions from rich countries would need to cultivate alliances heavily dependent on representatives from poor countries. Voting by houses over money bills and certain other matters would be a last-resort device for preventing the interests of rich countries, or of any large enough region or self-defining section of the world, from being completely overlooked. (There would need to be provisions for preventing it from paralysing the system.) But the formation of such a union governed by representatives chosen in proportion to population would still represent a big shift of influence toward poor countries, and rich-country representatives would be facing potent political pressures from the world body to release more finance for international redistribution.

But why would the people of rich countries *want* to enter governmental unions with poorer countries in which inevitably they would be under stronger pressure for sharing their material wealth? For the same kind of reasons presumably for which the affluent founders of the European Community/Union were keen to incorporate first the poorer lands of Southern Europe, then the very much poorer 'transition' countries of East-Central Europe – with an eye on Turkey and even on Ukraine (its population as big as France's and possibly about as poor as China's). Each successive batch is likely to make fresh demands for transfers from the richer members, and each makes the structures of the Union harder to operate and undermines sacred cows such as the Common Agricultural Policy. Yet they are invited in, no doubt from a mixture of motives: sentiment; genuine goodwill; long-term and rather visionary hopes of material gains all round; a handle on environmental pollution; and (much more important probably) a desire for political stability and peace in the region. *Mutatis mutandis*, similar motives might inspire the richer countries to promote an even wider union, and reasons not entirely different from those of the East-Central Europeans and Turkey might prompt other middle- and low-income countries to be keen to join.

Even in the absence of a governmental union, there might still be bases for taxes, or other sources of revenue, that could be counted as international and might consequently have much of their proceeds directed to global public purposes including the fight against poverty. Some of these might be politically less costly or embarrassing to the governments that would have to consent to their use than an agreed system of national contributions based on ordinary domestic revenue. These possibilities will be explored in Chapter 5.

Prospects of significant revenue sources such as this (applied through purely and directly consensual arrangements among states), however, are not firm and reliable enough to weaken the case for movement toward some form of governmental union. Conversely, governmental union is far from being a near enough prospect to justify any slackness in pursuing *other* devices for channelling more resources toward the mitigation of poverty in countries of lowish income.

Environmental protection

Global warming, to take up another theme broached in Chapter 2, is a striking example both of the potentially harmful effects that arise accidentally from human activity and of those that might be averted by co-ordinated action. Attempts to deal with it since around 1990 illustrate the difficulties of making an appropriate global response to such ubiquitous environmental challenges by consensual means. As time goes on, it seems quite likely that our propensity for generating unintended but serious outcomes, and also our technical capacity for protecting our species and its environment if we work together, will increase. Today it is global warming. In a few decades it may be pressure on usable fresh-water supplies. A century or more hence we might be threatened with the impact of a large meteor – or global cooling. Each of these events is a challenge to both prevention and adjustment. Global warming itself may lead to flooding of densely inhabited areas – or alternatively, possibly simultaneously, to desertification – and any of these events may demand resettlement of people at huge financial and political costs. To meet preventative and mopping-up tasks of this order, we shall need to have a capacity for co-ordinated restraint and for mobilizing resources on at least a respectable fraction of the scale of the resources commonly mobilized for a major war.

Can we expect this from an agency or convention or club? Dealing with these threats is likely to entail palpable sacrifices, often for delayed and even debatable benefits. We have seen all the plausible reasons advanced for arguing that the global-warming effect does not exist or that if it does it is harmless.

There may perhaps be serious debate over whether the *extent* of potential harm justifies the cost of limiting general warming through the very imperfect mechanism specified under the Kyoto Protocol, or even through an improved and more comprehensive version of national targets along the same lines. (See Lomborg 2001: 258–324.) But such debate needs to take account of the large element of uncertainty about the effects; the extent to which some of them may be practically irreversible; and the distribution across the world of likely benefits and costs – with the difficulty of using the benefits to compensate those who suffer the costs, and the expectation that the costs will be concentrated in poorer countries.

Even now, when governments and prevailing opinion have mostly accepted the reality of the effect and the need for action, any hope of a response commensurate with the threat as generally perceived is emerging slowly and uncertainly at best. The brittle and untidy half-consensus on a system reached at Kyoto in 1997, with so much still to be filled in, seemed itself a near-miracle in view of the mutually exclusive positions taken up in advance by the various groups of countries in their supposed interests. Prestige, and fear of being out-manoeuvred – all related to the fixation on supposed national interests – blocked what seemed sensible arrangements (Grubb et al. 1999: ch. 3, especially 109–11). And then in March 2001 the agreement was explicitly abandoned by the US, the biggest contributor by far to global warming (*Keesing*: 44082). In spite of the possibility in principle of an acceptable and workable agreement, outlined below in Chapter 5, a conclusion difficult to escape is that very probably for this purpose, and quite possibly for the meeting of some other important environmental challenges, a governmental union – one that brings other benefits, such as the large bonus of cut-price security, in exchange for surrender of the capacity to free-load on environmental restraints – is the only satisfactory resting-place.

Again, this can of course not be a pretext for failing to explore every other avenue in the meantime.

Human rights

Here there is already a convention over half a century old, the Universal Declaration of Human Rights, and there are other subsequent conventions filling the gaps. Yet, according to Amnesty International, at least 125 countries still recently practised torture and at least 47 performed extrajudicial executions (*Amnesty* 99, January–February 2000: 14). There are huge obstacles of interest, prejudice, and prestige to remedying these abuses or even admitting that they exist. Sources of moral pressure from within are often simply suppressed. Moral pressure from without may work in individual cases but still have little impact on institutions.

What is needed is a right of legal action against any government before a supranational tribunal (such as exists, within member-countries of the Council of Europe, to the European Commission on, and Court of, Human Rights), with effective channels for exercising that right and machinery for enforcing it.

Change is likely to come only if advantages of some kind, material or symbolic, broadly shared by those in power, go with it. While there might be *ad hoc* consensual deals that (implicitly if not explicitly) gave poorer countries financial benefits in exchange for participating in an effective human-rights regime, and further elaboration of international investigating agencies and tribunals might add to the moral pressure for good behaviour, these devices might well prove a long way from adequate, and the only solid hope (or at least, in spite of the inevitable delay, the quickest hope) of reaching a roughly suitable arrangement may be through the complex of reciprocal and shared benefits that could be attached to a governmental union.

While governments have the effective and ostensibly legitimate power to abuse, many of them will do so, occasionally if not regularly, by failures in vigilance if not through deliberate policy. Those that care about justifying themselves will find grounds for treating their own cases as special, as has been exemplified since 2001 by the semi-official endorsement on the part of the United States of the use of torture and by the excuses the US government has offered for its practice of arbitrary imprisonment and denial of due process. To make the surrender of the power and the ostensible legitimacy sufficiently attractive to potentially abusive governments or their controlling constituencies, a governmental union must have compensating benefits to offer. The particular governmental union – by its constitution, by its character, by its own performance hitherto or that of its nearest precursors – will also need to assure public opinion among those populations who care about such things that it will on balance provide a scourge rather than a shelter for abuse. 'Any old governmental union' will not do. The process by which the union is formed and extended will have to be such as to compensate and reassure those whose consent to its formation and extension is needed.

Peace

For keeping the peace, there is likely to be no satisfactory solution short of a governmental union. This was recognized by reputable wise persons at the end of the Second World War.[3]

If there are consensual rules purporting to determine when warfare is legitimate, armed states are always likely to find reasons for infringing them. And rules will in any case need an interpreter to determine their implications for particular situations. It is also probably unrealistic to suppose that this interpretation can be simply a judicial process. The interpreter will have to be an authority making what are essentially political decisions, a body more like the Security Council than like the World Court. That would raise the question of the authority's legitimacy. If the Security Council has no effective powers of enforcement, its moral claim to be the world's executive in matters of peace and war may not be strong enough to do the job: to make it an effective world-government-substitute.

Try as we may and should to find a way of giving the Security Council the moral authority to make up for its substantial lack of enforcement power, we may readily conclude that another approach is also needed. We need to find a way of building towards an authority that does have powers of enforcement – probably a monopoly of weapons of war – with the essential preconditions that (a) its constitution is such as to give it as much moral authority as a constitution can give, and that (b) it emerges from an entity whose *performance* reassures those that need to be reassured. Stating the latter precondition this way implies that a world governmental union of the kind needed – indeed of the only kind that we might expect to be formed by consent rather than conquest – must come about by building up gradually from embryonic beginnings: from a much smaller association that has managed to combine diverse nations and previously independent states voluntarily in a union of governmental character.

While some of the threats that were perceived in the 1950s may have diminished (since 1990 at least, it has seemed unlikely that any of the protagonists of the two World Wars will fight one another again in the near future), the problem has grown in other ways. There are now far more independent countries; there are more nuclear powers, with no convincing cap on their number; and much of the fighting of the second half of the twentieth century has sprung from insurgent movements within recognized states. Where there are wars between states, these are often connected to what is seen as domestic oppression, or they result from one party's siding with a domestic faction in the territory of another. Simple interstate aggression comparable to what preceded the Second World War, such as Iraq's attacks on Iran and Kuwait, or wars over borders, such as that in the late 1990s between Ethiopia and Eritrea, are if anything the exceptions.

This last feature might seem at first glance to weaken the hopes that might be placed in a governmental union. Admittedly, the idea that a world association or authority possessed of overwhelming military forces – far more than any component state – would thereby necessarily be able to keep a universal peace no longer seems as obvious as it may once have done. Insurgents without command of state machinery can resist the greatest military powers – as Vietnam, Afghanistan, and Chechnya have shown. Peacemaking by a world authority would inevitably involve the complicated business of interference in 'domestic' affairs: seeking to right wrongs or perceived wrongs, promoting territorial changes, rebuilding, resettling.

So a union that has any chance of generally keeping and restoring peace will need not only command over military forces – probably an 'official' monopoly over certain kinds of weapon – but also a recognized right to raise and to pursue questions of group claims to fair treatment and to cultural autonomy, and to rearrangement of state boundaries; and regular and respected procedures for seeking settlement of disputes over such matters. It goes without saying that the solutions will not be easy and that a heavy-handed approach could easily be disastrous. In many situations there are neither appeals to universal rules of justice nor exercises of superior force that can guarantee sustainable peace.

So the formation of a world governmental union – even a 'true' confederation with an official monopoly of highly destructive weapons, one that is subject to constitutional processes to which all the governments have freely consented – will not by itself guarantee an and to fighting. Unofficial conflicts may continue.

Yet this does not mean that governmental union is any less relevant to the business of keeping the peace. What it means is that other developments – both of interstate law and of dispute-settling procedures – beside political ingenuity, will also be needed. It may be in fact that the extension of any such true confederation to cover much of the world will have to be preceded or at least accompanied by changes in interstate laws and mores, under which (a) boundaries are recognized as adjustable and (b) claims of certain types put forward by groups within a state are submitted to standardized procedures of international mediation, conciliation, and arbitration. (These possibilities are discussed in Chapter 7.) But, even if that is so, reinforcing this behaviour, and upholding the formal institutions on which it depends, will be easier once there is a single, democratically limited, authority controlling the armaments.

Finding institutions for securing world peace must be a complex process of interconnected moves. Yet pooling the weapons and military forces in a sufficiently trusted constitutional union – which is what a true confederation involves – must surely be one critical component, a necessary element, and its universal accomplishment one of the long-term goals.

***

Attacking extreme poverty, environmental protection, safeguarding human rights, preserving peace: these objectives will have significant costs, material or symbolic, for important parties. They are unlikely to be achieved to the extent that the people of the world need them without governmental union, designed so that it can reflect in action common interests and concerns.

Yet peoples, as represented by their governments, would need to be drawn voluntarily into such a union, one that might in certain circumstances, over particular issues, override their own interests as they perceived them. There would need to be some general belief that the gains were likely to outweigh the losses. Also, as we have seen, the process would almost certainly have to be a gradual one, under which states were drawn in one by one to an evolving entity. This is not in principle impossible, but bringing it about universally will require a strategy, some concept of a process through which it might happen.

Fortunately there is an institution in existence that has shown the process in action and that also seems to be a potential vehicle for carrying it forward.

Summary of Chapter 3

- States may act together through *consensual unions*, each of which is either not licensed to override or replace any national-government decisions at all, or is allowed to do so only over a specific and limited area of subject-matter and under some form of consensual or majority decision by participating governments.

- Alternatively, they may act through *governmental unions*, in which (a) a range of different subject-matters can be embraced by a single set of institutions; (b) there is an executive empowered to take action across the range in ways that go beyond the interpretation of specific rules; and (c) decisions on rules and policy are not necessarily the province solely of member-state governments.

- Where an area of policy is one in which the necessary joint action to be taken by the world does not require palpable sacrifices, even over the fairly short term, on the part of any significant constituency, a consensual union may well be adequate. Trying to proceed to a governmental arrangement while there are plausible possibilities of meeting needs through consensual union – possibilities that have not clearly been exhausted and proved inadequate – is to raise unnecessary obstacles to the venture of giving the world the autonomy it needs.

- Further joint action needed globally for *economic stabilization* (as through international compensatory finance, sovereign-debt management, or social-insurance); for the co-ordination of national revenue-raising in order to make it watertight and not mutually undermining; and for devising acceptable approaches to open world trade: all this has the potential to be adequately covered by consensual unions (agencies, conventions, clubs, or voluntary tribunals). In all three cases, there are further strong reasons against passing control to a single global authority, whatever its democratic credentials.

- However, raising revenue for global disposal in order to fulfil the requirements of world social justice through the attack on extreme poverty; global environmental protection; the consistent safeguarding of basic human rights; and the maintenance of peace: these are all likely to demand progress to *governmental union*. In order to minimize the obstacles, the union should be thought of as a *confederation* – which members are free to leave – rather than as a *federation* depending on irrevocable surrender of sovereignty. Confederal powers sought should be the least that are needed to meet the purposes of the union, and the representatives of groups of nations may need to be given a veto on certain matters in order to ensure that their interests are not too injuriously overridden.

- But the process of reaching the governmental unions required to meet these needs may be long and uncertain. In the meantime, what consensual unions can do to fill the gaps should be pushed as far as it will go.

- Whether unions are consensual or governmental, states and their peoples will need to be persuaded to enter willingly. If they are to join in a governmental union, there must be perceived gains to themselves or the causes they value in order to compensate for the powers of independent action that they surrender. They will need reassurance over the character of the association that they are joining. Once inside they will need reassurance over the effects of admitting further members. This means that the process of moving toward global governmental union will inevitably be a gradual one, building from small beginnings.

● There is an institution in being that shows us how this might happen. The institution also seems fit to serve as a vehicle for bringing it about.

Notes

1. The Zedillo 'High Level Panel', appointed by the UN Secretary-General and reporting in June 2001, proposed consideration of the case for an international tax organization with a number of possible functions (UN 2001: 9, 64–6), very much as argued earlier by Vito Tanzi (1996: 12, 13).

2. There is also a large gap between current and prospective efforts on the one hand and on the other the World Bank estimates (provided to the Monterrey Summit on Financing for Development in 2002) of what would be necessary to achieve the UN General Assembly's Millennium Development Goals by 2015 (Devarajan et al. 2002). The estimated need of extra aid would be of the order of $50–60 billion a year, which would entail roughly doubling the current level of Official Development Assistance.

3. See Maritain (1954: ch. 7), where he cites the views of a number of respected thinkers at the time and their joint attempts to drive the idea forward.

Chapter 4

The European Union: a vehicle ready to hand

Our argument so far has been that a limited world governmental union is a necessary element in the accomplishment of four critical objectives that must be pursued for the sake of a safe, humane, prudent, responsible world society.

Yet we recognized the intrinsic difficulty of bringing such a union about: that peoples and states would need convincing that what they could gain from a union would outweigh the losses of independence in certain matters that it would entail. They would need to be reassured, probably by experience rather than simply argument. Even if the objective conditions for an acceptable union had been achieved – a difficult enough requirement in itself – we should still have to be persuaded that this had happened.

We need, if not a roadmap, at least a broad strategy for reaching the goal.

Core of the strategy: progressive widening and deepening

The European movement of the second half of the last century – most strikingly, though not solely, embodied in the organization now called the European Union – has shown in practice how the process can be carried forward: by progressive widening and deepening.

'Widening' means adding new members. 'Deepening' covers one or both of two movements: increasing the range of subjects covered by the Union, and increasing the extent to which they are decided by specifically Union institutions – as against such state-based elements as requiring a consensus among state governments so that each of those governments individually retains a veto. Each new step of widening or deepening allows the public in the member-countries to judge whether the situation so created is really on the way to becoming intolerable or whether there are even possibly gains on balance.

On reflection we can see that this is probably the only way that union of this kind – a wide-ranging association that has some of the key characteristics of a government – can emerge by voluntary agreement. People cannot be expected to take a huge leap into the unknown. The easiest steps in both widening and deepening have to be taken first. The two elements have to be paced. Too much deepening of the wrong sort may preclude or delay further widening. A bout of widening may rule out certain forms of deepening.

It will help if a long-term goal, even a provisional one, is clear and accepted, so that widening, and especially deepening, are not pursued indiscriminately, as if for their own sakes. It is an important element of the message here that deepening – for the world, and even for an area such as Europe considered on its own – should and probably can go only so far.

There is no guarantee, of course, that a process of progressive widening and deepening, however cleverly pursued, will reach the goal: as advanced here, a democratic world governmental union in a few essentials. But it is pretty clear that a goal of this sort will not be achieved without it. For this purpose it is the only game in town.

The vehicle as well?

European union is the demonstration case. Can it also be the vehicle? At first sight, this may seem an odd jump. Why should a European union develop into a world union? Looked at from the European end and without account of what has actually been going on in the wider world and what the world needs, there is no obvious reason. Probably most of the people who have been enthusiasts for the European movement during its first half-century have not seen this as its destiny.

Yet, if we start from the other end – from the need of the world for a governmental union, perhaps even for the sake of our species' survival – the judgement can surely be different. The unavoidable strategy of progressive widening and deepening means that the movement must start somewhere. And where better to start than where it has already started – and already proceeded some distance? Moreover the European movement's experience, which might well have amazed the architects of the

Treaty of Rome if they could have foreseen it back in the 1950s, is that there is a queue to join, even after the big accession of 2004, and also that not all the postulants are unambiguously part of Europe. Turkey, Muslim in tradition and bordering on the Caucasus and Syria and Iraq, looks very likely to enter in the century's first decade or soon after. And not very far back in the minds of those who think about these things must be the Ukraine and Russia – Russia, with a territory that extends to the easternmost point of Asia and borders China, raising the not-very-remote possibility of a union stretching from the extreme east to the extreme west of the Eurasian landmass.

All impossible of course, as, twenty years before this book was written, were so many of those things that we now take for granted: a united Germany, former Politburo members heading NATO countries, and an EU extending to the gates of the (then long-vanished) city of St Petersburg. What has happened to Europe has run ahead of our imaginations. And, within that turmoil of events, the entity that has become the European Union has itself moved in a mysterious way.

Why now a rolling snowball?

The EU has come to resemble a rolling snowball. Why are its neighbours so keen to join? First, as the new prospective members are all relatively poor, there is some prospect of economic aid. But that in itself probably does not count for much. Then there is trade: a guaranteed free entry to what may soon be the world's biggest fully unified market for goods and capital. Sensibly, the candidates seem undeterred by the fact that their own markets must also be open. (And, for well or ill, the worst feature of the Union, the Common Agricultural Policy, can seem a convenient milch-cow.) Then – perhaps rightly from their point of view, perhaps not in some cases – most are probably glad at the prospect of embracing the euro. It gives an apparent anchor for price stability. Provided their own internal relative prices remain flexible, it may be on balance a gain, especially if they would otherwise be prone to fiscal and monetary indiscipline. And the euro contributes to another advantage: economic respectability. Not only will there be a guarantee of free capital movement to and from Western Europe. In addition, some of the perceived risk to foreign investors, particularly from exchange-rate variation and other possibilities, will be reduced. Possibly also of some importance still for the 2004 crop of new entrants has been the prospect of joining a distinguished club, and for their ministers of sitting at a top table. This attraction will presumably wane as the number of members increases. But there is also implied political and defence support: quite relevant in Eastern Europe where memories of being overrun and destructively dominated for much of the twentieth century are still fresh.

It is obviously an advantage, on many of these scores, that the European Union was initially a club of the rich and relatively stable, with a wealthy core that has been economically very large, even in comparison with the 2004 batch of entrants. Not all these attractive features will continue undiminished as the union expands. But there is a reasonable prospect that the elements of economic respectability and implied political and defence support will continue to be important, and that new members will continue to recognize a positive balance of advantage from the open-trade regime. As the size of the Union increases in relation to that of the rest of the world, the confidence to be derived from its political and defence support will surely increase, even if the need for it eventually diminishes.

But why let them in?

Why are the existing members – rich, stable, and self-satisfied – so ready to open the doors of their club to the relatively poor, relatively precarious, less established national societies of the east and south? This is not a new phenomenon. Ireland, Greece, Spain, and Portugal were all relatively poor when they were admitted. Financially they were net recipients, like the new members of 2004. What motivates this enthusiasm for accepting an economic burden? We can speculate about the answer, but the important fact is that the disposition exists.

Perhaps the most important thing to say is that 'Europe' has become a vision, with which some people at least have become engaged. They care about the prosperity, the influence, the harmony of Europe, as citizens commonly do about their own 'national' societies. We do not bother to ask ourselves what materially we gain from our own country's harmony and prosperity. It simply goes without saying that these things matter.

But alongside this sentiment, and also part of the motivation of the European movement from the first, was a strong desire to preserve peace in the long term. This was coloured in the early days of the movement by the perceived threat from the Soviet Union, a danger thought to be aggravated by any internal economic weakness or inter-state strife in the West. But beside this there was a desire to bind the states together in mutual dependence, so as to prevent them from ever again fighting each other. Circumstances now are not exactly the same, but similar concern about the risks of warfare among the newly 'liberated' national states of Eastern Europe was understandable in the 1990s – the decade of Croatia and Bosnia and Kosovo – as was residual uneasiness about Russia.

Not entirely unconnected with these previous two motives has been a desire to encourage democracy and a liberal respect for individual human rights. Greece, Spain, and Portugal were admitted not long after they released themselves from their dictatorships. Spain and Portugal had been refused Association Agreements while they were under the regimes founded by Franco and Salazar, and Greece's Agreement was 'frozen' during the rule of the Colonels (Bainbridge 2002: 158–9). A desire to give moral support to democracy and human rights cannot be ruled out. Apart from what value these practices among our neighbours can have for the rest of us, we tend to think that they are also good in themselves.

Another motive at the beginning was a desire for economic emulation of the US – through a large internal market – or for economic bargaining-power vis-à-vis the US – through bigger international weight. And these Europe-centred aspirations were fortified in some minds by more traditionally liberal ideals of open trade. There are interesting individual cases of support for aspects of union – such as that of a forceful and long-running British Prime Minister who will probably go down in history as a profound eurosceptic. Not not only was she keen on widening because of a vision of the Union as an area of free trade and factor movement which should in her view be as extensive as possible, but also, on the side of deepening, she was prepared to accept the Single European Act of 1986 in the belief that this was necessary to make the market genuinely open. Maybe one kind of backer for union on grounds of economic efficiency and vigour might have been satisfied with the 'rich' EU of say 1995 or even 1973. Another would go for continuing enlargement.

Of course, those individuals whose lives and careers are closely tied to European union have a natural tendency to advance it. Hostile comment sometimes implies that this is the only reason the advance occurs. But there are abundant opportunities for national governments to block these developments if that is what they want or what they think their people want. If the 'eurocrats' were the only ones who wanted expansion of membership or intensification of union, it would not happen.

And we in the older, richer member-states do not seem to have been worried at the prospect of net subsidization to be extended to the new entrants of the 1980s and 2004. Either we are positively happy about it, or we consider the cost outweighed by the advantages of expansion. It seems we are prepared to pay – if not for the sake of some degree of fraternal equalization with our neighbours on its own account, then at least for encouraging democracy and the observance of human rights, or for increased long-term prospects of peace, or for the triumph of the European project.

But are we likely to stay where we are: to close ranks after the entries of 2004 or soon after, and to accept the present arrangements as a *de facto* constitution, regardless of what actually emerges from the constitutional discussions and proposals of 2002–4?

Will widening and deepening be carried further?

Widening

Expansion policies – present and past – suggest that the populations and leaders of current EU members, most of them among the world's rich, *do* on the whole care about democracy and human rights and long-term peace prospects. They see gain on balance rather than loss from expanded markets. And they are prepared to pay at least a little on these accounts.

If so – and it is not just an exclusive preoccupation with the romantic idea of Europe that motivates them – then there is good reason to expect that they will be prepared to go on widening. If further candidates meet the political and (loose) economic criteria set, and seem able and willing to enact and enforce the Union's rules, and there is no obvious reason in the character of their societies and governments telling *against* membership, they will sooner or later be admitted. Where on the face of the world they happen to lie – especially which side of arbitrary lines on maps – will cease to matter.

At first, it is likely to be those on the European periphery who apply, so that there will be no call to sacrifice too many sacred cows at once. Turkey was accepted as an applicant in 1999 (Bainbridge 2002:

157) and in December 2004 accession talks were authorized. Like the Roman Empire, 'Europe' may fairly soon come to be extended to the Tigris and Euphrates, and psychologically it is only a small step from there to Kamchatka and the shores of the Bering Strait.

Turkey can be a wedge case. The AK government, fairly newly in power at the time of writing, has been prepared to deal with the (big) issue of human rights and it has also done its best over the division of Cyprus – grievances that have been major blocks to Turkey's entry. As soon as these matters are convincingly settled and it also becomes apparent that the generals have given up the belief in their entitlement to intervene forcibly in the political process, there will be no further important obstacles, at least none where the objections are respectable enough to be spoken openly. Once the Bosphorus barrier is broken – once Asia Minor is part of Europe – it may dawn on us that geography, especially its artificial divisions, should not be a determining factor.

The membership of Turkey can also help to dispel another hang-up: the idea that a rich country cannot in its own interest form a common market in goods and services with a much poorer one. Turkey is close to the poor end of the line-up of recent entrants and current applicants and is also big enough to be a test case. The presumption that free trade between rich and poor is harmful to either side conflicts with one of the most fundamental insights of the economics of the last two centuries. Canada and the US and Mexico have defied this piece of folklore in forming the North American Free Trade Agreement. As in any expansion of competition, there will be people and industries disturbed by these arrangements, and there will always be questions over how far the opening should be gradual and what exceptions should be permitted. But poor–rich competition is no less intrinsically likely to be beneficial (to both sides), once initial disturbances have passed, than rich–rich or poor–poor competition, and no more intrinsically likely to leave resources temporarily unemployed.

Briefly, take away a few prejudices, taboos, and misapprehensions, and there is little reason why what has impelled the European Union and its predecessors to welcome successive waves of new members (since 1980 mostly poorer) should not lead it to go further, far beyond that western enclave of the Eurasian landmass that was once Latin Christendom. And it may take Turkey to break the spell.

There is no reason to expect the flow of candidates to dry up. And, if the relevant mental blocks are shifted, the Union may come round to admitting them provided only that they meet entry conditions relating to broad political characteristics of their societies and practice. (Whether relaxing certain features of the EU itself would make it easier to remove the obstacles will be discussed below.)

Deepening

The EU is unlike conventional federations on the US pattern. They have a fairly clear constitutional division of powers and functions, so that, though the pattern of effective authority can change – through rare constitutional amendments, exceptional judicial decisions, and gradual developments of practice – it is stable for long periods. By contrast, the working constitution of the EU has been in a constant state of flux. It started as the framework for an association of one sort, but also in the minds of many of its founders as a strategy for achieving a very different form of union. Aspiration and fact have always been different. The constitution has had to satisfy as far as possible both those who want to stop where they are and those who want to move on toward a distant goal. So it is in practice designed for change. Whatever attempts are made to stabilize it, the strong likelihood is that the product that emerges from the constitutional discussions of 2002–4 will turn out in practice to be of the same plastic character. And from the standpoint of this book that is all to the good.

The two processes that comprise deepening present separate issues. On the question (1) of the subject-matter for confederal control (as distinct from co-ordination), it would be desirable (from the point of view advanced here) for a pressure-group, or even the main thrust of the European movement, to fix on a certain small range of matters to become effectively confederal, with confederal control over other possibles either deliberately excluded or treated pragmatically – to be considered, as occasion may arise, on their individual merits or as matters of national choice. The key items in the list, however, would include those of the greatest political difficulty: most notably a power over defence and foreign policy, and hence necessarily a significant independent power of taxation.

It seems likely in fact that, failing some fairly radical change in perceptions, the forces acting on the EU will not push it toward a clearly defined goal. The Union role on several matters will continue to hang somewhere between co-ordination and control, with the possibility of further movement in the control direction. There will be forces for and against confederalizing several important powers, and there will often be reasonable cases to be made on both sides.

The institutions of the Union will continue to make a useful co-ordinating framework for much that will be unsuitable as subject-matter of union authority, and we can expect the range of subjects of joint interest to continue expanding as technological and other changes throw up new problems that need to be faced jointly. But much of this new matter may be best kept in the consensual box, for co-ordination and no more.

'Deepening' also covers (2) the separate but related process of removing or reducing national vetoes and intergovernmental decision-making on matters agreed to be confederal, and instead construct-ing institutions so that a view on them is likely to be taken from the standpoint of the whole rather than simply as a compromise among national interests as viewed by state governments. What can be said about experience to date is that the EU and its predecessors have moved bit by bit in this direction. Authority has been divided among 'the Council' (a term used here to cover both the Council of Ministers and the European Council), the Commission, and the Parliament – the Council, representing governments, acting as the senior partner, though with considerable opportunities for influence in the hands of the Commission. The Commission and the Parliament are inclined to think in 'community' terms – both, and especially the Commission, intrinsically inclined to increase the effective powers of the Union, as well as their own powers as specifically Union institutions – with the Council forming a counterweight. From the starting-point, when nothing much resembling a parliament existed, there has been progres-sive reduction of the scope of governmental veto power in the Council, and increasing, though still limited, authority for the Parliament.

On the assumption of reasonable tranquillity, it seems likely that this form of deepening will continue, though entry of new members that carry considerable weight (together or individually) may slow it or halt it until enough mutual confidence between old and new members is attained.

There is likely to be interaction between the two forms of deepen-ing, and it is not necessarily the case that advance in one will tend to limit advance in the other. Sometimes deepening of the one form will be encouraged by, or be essential to, deepening in the other. It is hard, for example, to see a genuine community foreign policy developing unless there is a single executive and an effective legislature, both with clear pan-Union democratic credentials.

★★★

The conclusion from this speculation on the future tendencies of the Union is that, even without a clear deliberate direction of change toward a specific world role such as this book is advocating, widening (beyond the arbitrary borders of Europe) and deepening (in at least the latter of the two senses) are likely to continue. The plea of this book is that these movements should be consciously directed toward goals that will exploit the Union's potential for promoting peace, justice, and security across the world.

The impact of entry conditions

Thoughts of a world union may naturally lead some of us in the present EU to wonder how we could ever consent to be closely tied, politically or economically, to more than a handful of the existing states that are now outside it. Make the entry conditions tough enough to exclude those we could not possibly work with, it might seem, and we shall find there are few eligible candidates.

That may describe the situation as it is. But the world is changing. In Europe itself since 1970, there has been tremendous progress in the realm of democracy, human rights, and the rule of law. Take 1980 as the starting-point, and the same has been true of Latin America generally (Brazil, Argentina, Chile, Guatemala, arguably also Mexico, Uruguay, Peru), the Philippines, South Korea, Taiwan. For all the disappointments in sub-Saharan Africa, there have been huge changes of the whole style of regime since 1990 in South Africa and Ethiopia – with two of the four largest populations in the region – and movement in the right direction for the state with the largest numbers, Nigeria, and for Mozambique and Malawi and Kenya. In spite of the difficulties and imperfections of democracy among the fifth of the world's population living in South Asia, it has kept its foothold in India, Bangladesh, and Sri Lanka, and intermittently in Pakistan and Nepal. Indonesia too, with the world's fourth-largest population, moved around the turn of the millennium in a decidedly democratic direction.

The emphasis on democracy and liberal immunities, however, conceals another implied requirement. Robert Cooper (1996) writes of the cross-border elements of governance that have developed most strikingly in Europe as characterizing the 'post-modern state'. But the post-modern state supposes the prior existence of the 'modern state', where there may be few cross-border elements but the government has effective control and can make laws and issue orders that are generally obeyed. When the modern state is at its most complete, the police and courts and bureaucracy will on the whole enforce and administer the law or at least coherent government policy. In much of the world (Cooper's 'pre-modern states'), this is only fitfully true – and in some of it scarcely true at all – and this sometimes in spite of the forms of democracy and substantial freedom of the press. Traditional leaders, landlords, generals, or the very rich, may be able to determine between them the outcomes of political processes (often very inefficient outcomes because they represent the result of competition and compromise among the particular private interests of relatively few people, or because positive-sum outcomes that would be made possible by effective government are unavailable), and also the extent and biases with which the law is enforced.

But again these deficiencies are not necessarily static and are capable of improvement. A society such as China in the 1920s that was in large part the preserve of rival warlords could progress in a few decades to something approaching a 'modern' state – in the sense of one in which the central government could to a considerable extent impose its will. And significant progress to free elections and the rule of law may often, as we've seen, take place over quite short periods.

A union based in Europe – or hypothetically in North America for that matter: in either of the two main centres of the affluent world – a union that much of the world eventually wants to join, has the potential for encouraging these movements by its policy on accession, tipping the scales toward formal democracy, and within democracies toward the effective rule of law and enforced respect for human rights. It is this process that we have surely seen at work in Turkey, possibly also in Slovakia and elsewhere.

We should be hoping to link up, not necessarily with the world as it is, but with the world as it might be, and as on the whole it is becoming, and as it may become more surely and quickly if we keep the conditional possibility of a link open. Twenty years earlier even the wildest imaginations would scarcely have marked out for EU membership any of the eight candidates on the mainland that joined in 2004.

Present entry conditions and their global applicability

Timothy Bainbridge (2002: 155) summarizes them as follows:

> The basic qualifications for full membership of the Union are
> that the applicant is a European state . . . , that it is able and
> willing to assume the political and economic obligations of
> membership, . . . and that it is a democracy in which human
> rights are respected and guaranteed . . .

Expressed in the Copenhagen criteria of 1993 (ibid.: 96), the requirements are:

> Stability of institutions guaranteeing democracy, the rule
> of law, human rights and respect for and protection of
> minorities; . . . a functioning market economy, as well as the
> capacity to cope with competitive pressure and market forces
> within the Union; [and] the ability to take on the obligations
> of membership, including adherence to the aims of political,
> economic and monetary union.

If for the moment the 'European-state' test is set on one side, these
fall into three groups: general political tests relating to the character
of institutions; general economic tests (loose, and subject to wide possibilities of interpretation); and readiness for conformity to specific
Union laws (most of them relating to the single market) and to pro-
fessed aspirations.

How well would these tests serve a union with a programme of
gradually uniting the world in an area of peace, sustainability and
justice?

The four general political tests (democracy, rule of law, human
rights, minority protection) are unexceptionable and surely essential. (The 'rule-of-law' test supposes of course that the laws can be
implemented.) All are implied by the Universal Declaration of Human
Rights, long accepted (on paper) by the members of the United
Nations, so that there can be no complaint that these reflect the peculiar values of a section of the world. It is difficult to imagine that the
present members would be content with a union that did not insist on
these characteristics; and, as mentioned, the tests have the potential for
improving practice in postulant states. We have to hope – and there is
good reason in recent experience for hoping – that the sphere where
these tests are met will be progressively extended.

The general economic tests probably boil down in practice to the presence of substantial market elements in the economy. (The bit about the capacity to cope with competitive pressures and market forces within the Union is hardly likely to prove an effective obstacle if the postulant wants to be a member and is willing and able to meet the single-market legislative requirements.) No 'national' economy today – possibly no economy ever in a governed state – is entirely market-driven. Most of those that would apply for membership and meet the other tests today could probably be counted as market-driven enough.

That leaves the test of readiness for single-market legislation, and the aspirations. The aspirations can perhaps be cynically dismissed since they cost nothing. But can the single-market as understood in the EU be a reasonable ideal and target for the world? I have to enter important reservations here on two scores (with an arguable third that can probably in fact be ignored), and recognize that I have to deal with them in some way if the main theme of this book is to be upheld.

One of these – as will be clear from what has already been said – is monetary union. Besides featuring in the aspirations, monetary union is commonly thought of as an essential for making the single market complete. There are a number of potential aspirants that might fit happily into monetary union with the bulk of Europe. Paradoxically it is the affluent social democracies, with their commonly rather inflexible labour markets (such as France, the Netherlands, Britain, and, markedly at the time of writing, Germany), that are likely to find most debilitating, and in fact destabilizing, a system of interest-rate management geared to suit the current circumstances in economies other than their own. They, or most of them, may be induced to continue putting up with the losses entailed, for better or for worse. Yet, unless the nature of the world economy has changed immensely in the meantime, it is hard to see the US or Japan sharing a currency and a monetary regime with Europe or with each other. And this reluctance may well rest on sound economic judgement.

The saving grace here is that – thanks to Denmark, Sweden, and Britain – the common currency with its common monetary-policy regime is not yet a *de facto* requirement. And, despite the rhetoric, Britain at least will probably stay out, at least for the next ten years. That does not overcome the problem but provides at least a foothold – a pretext, a precedent – for coping with it.

The second – even more fundamental – difficulty is the aspiration to free movement of labour. So long as there is a sharp division of the world into rich and poor, the rich will not accept unlimited free immigration. Fears of the extent and ill-effects of uncontrolled immigration may be exaggerated, but they will remain, and they will be understandable. So long as there is prejudice or potential prejudice among a host population against outsiders, to leave permanently open the possibility of an unlimited influx into any area of people with obviously different appearance and customs raises the spectre of civil disorder and strife. We may regret this and believe it ought not to be so, but regrets do not remove the popular fears or the real risks.

The Common Agricultural Policy (CAP) would have been a third stumbling-block. However, it is already in process of slow but radical change. Its system of output subsidies on particular products is shifting to one of bonuses for working areas of land. The 2004 enlargement punctured another hole in it, in that the new members were treated differently from the old. So, in an important departure from principle, cover for the agriculture of new members would appear to be negotiable. Enlargement may be killing the CAP, rather than the converse. Increasingly effective outside pressure exerted in the WTO may gradually cause remaining protective elements to disappear. Briefly, the CAP in any recognizable form seems doomed.

★★★

If the institutions of the European movement are to be used for carrying forward a world-scale programme of union, certain ostensible requirements lurking under the present entry conditions – for monetary union and a single labour market – will have in some way to be circumvented.

Variable geometry: a possible escape-hatch

The term 'variable geometry', as applied to the institutions of the European movement collectively (the EU, the Council of Europe, NATO, the European Economic Area (EEA), the Western European Union (WEU), the Organization for Security and Co-operation in Europe (OSCE)), refers to the fact that different groupings are associated for the various functions, some of the unions extending unapologetically beyond the Europe of anyone's definition. NATO and the EU overlap; WEU involves a common subset of each of them; NATO includes Canada and the US. The human rights regime of the Council of Europe (like the EEA) covers all the EU members and more besides. The OSCE embraces almost everyone, from the Bering Strait to the Bering Strait.

Even within the EU, there are inner circles. Euroland still (end-2004) omits Denmark, Sweden, and Britain. Ireland and Britain have an opt-out, and Denmark a partial opt-out, from the 'Schengen acquis', under which the member-states of the Union practise open borders toward one another over movement of people (Bainbridge 2002: 436).

Committed federalists of course deplore these exceptions, and do their best to see that new applicants are not given similar leeway. This is understandable: the fact that 'variable geometry', even within the EU itself, is possible and not obviously disastrous, with opt-outs on matters as momentous as the common currency, points to a viable alternative to the pure federalist vision. Like it or not, there can in reality be closer unions on particular matters, within the wider Union, without leading to the collapse of the whole venture. Co-operation among subgroups of members, even in areas covered by the Union's treaties, was in fact allowed by the Treaty of Amsterdam (1997), but only under strict limits, which were further tightened by the Treaty of Nice (2001) (Bainbridge 2002: 283–4). Yet there is federalist uneasiness about too much variable geometry.

However, the flexible untidiness of the overlapping arrangements in the wider movement has almost certainly made possible much more co-operation than could have resulted from an all-or-nothing approach. Ireland as a committed neutral could not have joined the EEC in the Cold War time if the economic community had been rigidly coextensive with a defence union. The economic community itself would not have got off the ground if its projectors had insisted that it could only exist on condition that it embodied all the members of the Council of Europe. The euro, for better or for worse, would probably not have come into being in the absence of the opt-outs for Denmark and Britain.

In short, maintenance and extension of flexibility in some form will probably be necessary if the Union is to embark seriously on fulfilling the role proposed for it here. Most potential applicants will probably value the *right* to adopt the euro on certain fairly clear conditions. On short-term considerations, a number may value access to the CAP – if it still exists. The new entrants of 2004, and those eight or nine accepted or presumed as next in the queue, are likely to value the prospect of free labour movement into the old EU heartland – for themselves, if not necessarily for subsequent entrants. On the other hand, some of the older members will be increasingly dubious about swelling the Union further if free movement of labour is to be a universal rule. Expanding as far as possible, and at the same time satisfying as many as possible with forms of union that are mutually acceptable, will call for the acceptance of variable geometry.

Yet this is only to accept what has already been happening within the EU itself. (1) The Common Agricultural Policy since the 2004 enlargement has arguably ceased to be common. (2) The Union, as already mentioned, has shown that it can operate without an obligation on all members to adopt the euro (and it is not obvious what great benefits would accrue to the euro participants from insisting that any additional candidates from south-eastern Europe or further afield should either adopt the euro or remain in outer darkness). And (3) that at some point the terms of labour movement should be negotiable for new members is surely not inconceivable or clearly monstrous. (In fact, movement for work of people from the new member-countries into a number of the old ones was being somewhat curtailed immediately after the enlargement of May 2004. And it seems to be assumed that Turkey, if admitted, would face at least a long period over which the movement of its workers to other parts of the Union would be limited.) If potential applicants rejected the terms of labour movement that they were offered and did not judge that the benefits arising from other aspects of union were sufficient nonetheless to make it attractive, they could remain outside. It is not obvious that all *would* reject any terms short of full freedom of movement.

How these variations might in practice be accommodated within the framework of the Union so as to make possible continuous extension covering the most important aspects will be touched on in Chapter 6. The draft Constitution of 2004 has some relevant provisions that will be mentioned in the Appendix to that chapter.

A two-tier union?

A two-tier union is a temptingly neat solution – almost as neat as a conventional federation. But it will not do, for several reasons.

The most important is that it would straitjacket the realization of diverse wants and needs. Taken in an obvious sense, it would mean that all members accept joint authority in a certain range of essentials, and that a subset (group A) accept it also in a second range, but that those outside group A (group B) are excluded from all the Union institutions governing this second range – open borders and a common currency, for example, to take two items on which there are current opt-outs. If they refuse to accept the Schengen agreement over borders, they may not enter the euro arrangements. Ireland would have to abandon border controls for EU entrants if it wanted to remain within Economic and Monetary Union. It is hard to see the sense in this other than as a second-worst way of satisfying the passion for neatness and uniformity. It would exclude certain countries from unions that they chose and were otherwise eligible to join, or else oblige them to take part unwillingly in others that were nevertheless considered inessential to the core Union agenda.

The second reason against it is that an explicitly two-tier union would tend to create a sense of first-class and second-class members: an inner and an outer circle.

Altogether the diverse choices and circumstances of the nations of Europe – let alone those of the world – require freer and more untidy arrangements if there is to be (a) general union on matters on which it is universally needed, and simultaneously (b) optimum development of particular unions that suit particular countries' desires and conditions.

Variable geometry – choose a better term if you can think of one – is likely to be always with us: and a good thing too.

A choice among three destinies

What is now the European Union, or the European movement propelling it, has had the potential for moving in any one of three directions, toward any one of three coherent ideals.

An expanding area of free trade and investment

One ideal, strictly 'economic', is simply the extension of an area – universal or as wide as possible – of free trade and free factor movement, what we can call the Thatcher vision. States would continue to function in most respects as they have always done, relying on armed forces, treaties, alliances, as ways of preserving their liberties and traditions and keeping their peoples secure. The Union would of course eventually abandon the highly and irrationally protective Common Agricultural Policy. It might also abandon monetary union as a universal aspiration and any common social policies. It would be a free-trade club, but, because of its originally more limited membership, a much more rigorous and consistent one than the World Trade Organization. The European human rights regime could continue to function under the Council of Europe, to which adherence might still be obligatory. The bureaucracy needed and the rules and tribunals serving the Union itself would be only those necessary to monitor or enforce the open-market regime (but the Single Market Project alerts us to the fact that integrating markets may entail much bureaucratic work and legislation in order that national regulations on such matters as safety and professional qualifications can become mutually consistent). Co-operation *ad hoc* among smaller or larger groups of European countries, or of others within the community, would not of course be excluded; and the UN family would remain for consensual functions covering the world.

A vision of this sort can be self-consistent, and, if we were back in the 1960s or even somewhat later, it might have been an effective option. But so much more has happened to the Union since then, most of it very unlikely to be reversed. And, given the difficulty that the actual European Union has in dropping the very costly Common Agricultural Policy, unpopular internally as it is and quite destructive to the rest of the world, there must be doubts whether a Europe-based free-trade project can do much for world trade that the WTO cannot. (Paradoxically, the Union's distinctive contribution to freeing trade and factor movement has been the massive co-ordination of regulations attained through the Single Market Project, and the need for new members to adopt this body of law and enforce it may even present a practical barrier to enlargement.) The ideal also gives little promise of contributing to the realization of world peace, since little if any warfare now arises from trade disputes. And it leaves world social justice, world human rights, and world environment questions to other hands – all reasonable enough if there is really no likelihood that a European union can contribute significantly to meeting these concerns.

A United States of Europe

The second vision is that of a United States of Europe, shaped after the North American pattern, a conventional federation on the 1787 model as that model has developed over the succeeding two centuries: 'a new nation' with a common loyalty overriding loyalties to the component states. It would aim to occupy a certain roughly contiguous area of the earth and gladly admit to membership applicants from that area, but it would not aspire to extend its geographical range beyond. It would probably hope for a certain uniformity of culture and outlook. The federal government would have a monopoly of armed forces within its territory and would have a single foreign policy. It would observe complete free trade and factor movement internally, but would retain the right to impose barriers against the rest of the world (and hence might keep the Common Agricultural Policy or similar high protection for farming). It would have a single currency and a single centre of macroeconomic management, and most of the powers and functions that federations generally have. To give it a name, we might call this the Delors vision.

This again can be made internally consistent. But there are in fact elements within the Union that are strongly averse to the idea of transferring their loyalty. There can also be a risk of transgressing the reasonable and generally life-enhancing demands of subsidiarity. Other things being equal, we are happier when as much as possible is decided near home. And in particular the centralization of monetary policy, and hence of a large slice of macroeconomic management, such as much of the actual EU has begun to experience already, may be positively counter-productive, contributing to the very imbalances that macroeconomic management is intended to relieve. This in turn may aggravate political tensions.

A strategy of adopting everything that makes for the semblance of a federal state might backfire. Contrary to a view that seems to be widespread if implicit in euroenthusiast circles, Union exercise of irrelevant powers may well queer the pitch for those powers that are necessary. It is not necessarily true that every increase of Union authority will contribute to making 'a more perfect union', if 'more perfect' means better adapted to human needs, or more acceptable. Centralization on principle – or because other federations do it – is not a good guiding rule.

Again, this approach does not in any clear way give prospects of contributing further to world peace – except insofar as interstate wars might otherwise arise in Europe – or to civil and social justice beyond European territory, or to the conditions for global environmental security.

A path to an autonomous world

The third ideal, the one advocated here, is that of the limited democratic world confederation designed to make the world in certain key respects *autonomous* – with the European Union, and to an extent the other entities of the wider European movement, serving together as the seed-crystal for bringing it into being. The Union, with this mission, would not have to ape past federations. The question asked about some new potential power or function, such as that of macroeconomic management, would not be: 'Is this a central function essential to a federal state?' but rather 'Is this likely to be so much more effectively and beneficently exercised under central control as to outweigh the advantages of leaving the ultimate authority over it to the component states?'

The union would not be aiming to proclaim itself a new nation with a new loyalty. Its task would not be to prove that it was exercising all the powers that a 'normal' federal state would have. Rather it would exert itself to prove that it was not exercising more powers than were necessary for important human purposes.

Acceptance of this third ideal, rather than either of the others, need not underrate what the European movement has accomplished in Europe already, or the value of its recent extension in Southern and Eastern Europe, or the further extensions to the extreme southeast that may well happen in the century's first decade. The movement and the institutions it has fathered may have contributed to keeping the peace in Western Europe and to maintaining the confidence of the democratic part of the continent in the face of the Soviet Empire and the surviving dictatorships. But, if so, it is not clear that pressing further toward a 'real' federation on the same territory is likely to be necessary or sufficient for securing further benefits of the same kind.

On the other hand, the EU (with the accompanying human rights regime of the Council of Europe and its members' experience of defence co-operation) is equipped, as no other entity now is, to be the institutional focus of the long, slow process of extending by voluntary agreement a legally fortified, democratically supervised domain of peace, justice, and environmental security to the uttermost parts of the earth.

This is not (as is emphasized in the previous and next chapters) to decry the potential role of the UN family. There are certain key roles that can best be performed by *ad hoc* consensual unions, or can only be performed by an association of states that is universal or nearly so, or both. And, even in fields where a measure of universal *government* is needed, we may have to do the best we can for the time being with consensual associations. On the other hand, there are functions that can only be performed adequately at the present time by a governmental form of union that is necessarily selective.

One function may need to be pursued by both methods at once: through a consensual union that will be imperfect in execution but universal in its cover; and also through a governmental union that will be more thorough but cover in the interim a smaller part of the world. The approaches should be complementary, neither of them excluding or devaluing the other.

Summary of Chapter 4

- If a limited world governmental union covering a few key areas is the target, we need a strategy for reaching it.

- The European movement has demonstrated the only way by which a goal of this sort can realistically be targeted: through progressive *widening* (admitting new members) and *deepening* (covering further fields of co-operation, or enhancing the extent to which the association acts as an autonomous entity, or both).

- The European Union has acquired an attractive power: most of its neighbours have been keen to join.

- From a variety of motives, the Union has also been ready to admit new members, quadrupling its number of participating states in a little over thirty years.

- It has been prepared to admit countries much poorer than the existing Union average. States are welcomed if the following four conditions are met: that they satisfy certain tests of political practice (democracy, rule of law, civil rights, respect for minorities); that their economic institutions meet some rather vague and elastic requirements; that they are prepared to observe EU laws, mainly related to the single market; and hitherto that they can claim to be in Europe.

- The willingness to widen seems likely to persist, unless a preoccupation with neatness, or an intoxication with the North American model, or a romantic ideal of Europe, causes arbitrary lines to be drawn.

- Deepening is also likely in any case to continue, in the connected senses of (a) increasing in some respects the range and the intensity of Union involvement, and (b) enhancing the confederal democratic elements, as against the powers of state governments, in its constitution.

- The argument here is that widening and deepening should be consciously directed toward goals that exploit the Union's potential for promoting general peace, justice, and security. For these purposes, it would be desirable for the European movement to fix as a goal on a small set of vital topics for fully democratic confederal control, with others either deliberately excluded or considered pragmatically or as optional extras.

- The entry tests currently applied (aside from the confinement of entrants so far to Europe), and the practices new entrants are expected to follow, would be unlikely to block the form of indefinite enlargement envisaged in this book (union with any reasonably stable country that observes democratic, law-guided, and human rights norms) – were it not for three elements of current EU law and aspiration. These are the Common Agricultural Policy, the commitment to a common currency, and the principle of a unified labour market.

- But (1) the Common Agricultural Policy, in anything like its original form, is doomed and can probably be allowed to die. (2) Admittedly, the common currency is for good reasons likely to be unacceptable to certain potential entrants; but it is *de facto* optional for existing members; while it remains so, there is a good chance that it will not be imposed consistently on new entrants if, after meeting the Maastricht criteria, they are unwilling to enter the monetary union. However, (3) there are also likely to be severe limits on how far completely free migration can be accepted between rich and poor countries. To make the indefinite expansion of the Union possible, this last aspiration in its absolute form would, for the foreseeable future, have to be modified, and the terms of labour movement made negotiable for potential new members.

- In other words, a measure of 'variable geometry' will have to be accepted, with the core of the Union's functions confined to certain key elements and the rest optional extras. The result would necessarily be more untidy than the expression 'a two-tier union' suggests.

- There are three possible visions of the Union's future: an ever-enlarging area of free trade and investment; a 'new nation' populating a conventional federal state with fixed geographical boundaries; or, as advanced here, a confederation strictly limited in its powers but unlimited in its geography, aimed at making the world *autonomous* in essential matters relating to peace, justice, and environmental security.

Chapter 5

Parallel role of the United Nations family

This chapter will emphasize that the theme here is most emphatically *not* that forms that may develop out of present European institutions are rivals to the UN family as instruments for dealing with global concerns.[1] In the immediate present, the UN route is far more important. It is rather that there are certain goals that must ultimately be reached – ultimately, not tomorrow, but the sooner the better – and, for these, entities that are in principle universal from the beginning, and therefore necessarily consensual, will for the most part not prove fully equal to the task.

The key challenges – keeping the peace, environmental security, enforcing human rights, and attacking extreme poverty – are critical *now* and must be met with whatever resources the world can bring itself to muster. The consensual intergovernmental system that has been constructed must be used and stretched and pushed as far as possible to serve these absolutely crucial purposes. Yet, if we rely solely and permanently on consensual arrangements, it is quite likely, in spite of all efforts at reform, that these concerns will continue to be inadequately met – over, say, the next century if we are spared. The human family will still lack the degree of autonomy that it needs: that capacity to act as an entity, in accord with what seem, from the viewpoint of the whole, the demands of common prudence and justice. That is why we need the alternative – the governmental approach – at the same time, in spite of the inevitable delay before it can bear much fruit.

It is tempting to think that the present consensual institutions – those of the UN family in the broadest sense – could themselves be manipulated into becoming governmental in the necessary areas. Again, maybe that should be attempted. Perhaps that attempt is a necessary part of the business of getting as much mileage as we can from the legacy of international devices that stems from the vision taken up by the victors of the Second World War. But the prospect of success may not be very good. Envisaging the conversion *en bloc*, however gradually, of the UN General Assembly and the Boards of the World Bank and the International Monetary Fund into generally accepted law-making parliaments, or a law-making parliament, demands greater feats of imagination, surely, than those demanded by the main vision of this book.

Nurturing the consensual institutions, and expanding their competence, on the one hand, and developing governmental institutions, on the other, have the same objectives: security and justice. The two endeavours need not in the least degree conflict. In the immediate future that concerns us, they will be complementary, and only to a limited degree substitutes for one another.

Chapter 3 listed some areas for which, ultimately, consensual associations among governments are likely to be adequate – and also on the whole preferable. This chapter considers the four main areas (five if we include the necessary finance as a separate item) for which that chapter argued that consensual (intergovernmental) approaches are *not* likely to be fully sufficient but must nevertheless be fostered and developed as our main immediate source of remedies. It mentions a few of the ways in which these approaches may well be carried further than they have been so far, with synergies in some cases between them and the governmental project.

The link between universality and consensuality

The institutions of the UN family are *consensual*, as distinct from governmental, in the senses defined in Chapter 3. They are also for the most part *universal*, at least in principle: that is to say, most of them have no strong entry conditions, often no genuine entry conditions other than a willingness to make a financial contribution – at least nothing corresponding to the entry conditions for the EU. Some have been clubs, like the International Monetary Fund until 1971 and GATT/WTO, but in each of those cases entrants have had simply to state their willingness, and in the latter case to show their capacity, to observe the rules of the club, not to demonstrate comprehensive characteristics of their polities or economies.

The universality and consensuality go together. Because any and every state may be a member, and the aim is to include all significant players forthwith, the members can be expected to make only *ad hoc* and provisional commitments to each other. They cannot be expected to embrace general commitments, even unilaterally terminable commitments, to be ruled by any kind of joint majority decision over a range of important functions. Before taking that further step each would have to be satisfied with the general character of the others with whom its lot was to be cast. Those initially joining would need some trust in each other; and subsequent postulants for membership would need to be approved.

The question that must fix the brief for the central UN Organization and for each of the Specialized Agencies and the Bretton Woods Institutions (the World Bank Group and the IMF) is: on what useful constitution and principles can more or less everyone be expected to agree *now*? The 'more or less' is added because not quite everyone did always agree. There have been significant gaps, especially for a long time in the BWIs. Unanimity was not of course required for each decision and act. But the basis, the rules, had to be approved by all who joined. And it was taken as of great importance for the UN itself that everyone should join: initially, all those counted as on the Chinese–British–French–Soviet–American side or neutral in the Second World War; later, former enemies too and the legions of nations, great and small, that came to independence in the years that followed.

Both advantages and drawbacks arise from this universal–consensual character of the UN family. Advantages are that it can express a current world verdict or aspiration; that, when unanimous or nearly so, or representing broad agreement among its members, it can be regarded as neutral, more credibly so than any one government or alliance or interest-group of governments; that it can provide a permanent milieu for face-to-face diplomatic negotiation within whatever subgroup of states happens to be relevant, and a standing body for dealing with emergencies of any sort, natural or human in origin, anywhere; that it has a possibility of access for purposes of public service to the whole of the world's human capacities; that it has the potential for making use of resources that can only be mobilized in common, or for regulating access to resources where only universal rules of access will serve; and that the near-universality that it possesses is essential for the effective pursuit of some unequivocally global public-goods or public purposes.

Drawbacks faced by the actual UN family, largely following from its universal–consensual character, are that there is a bias toward inertia in its structures, because it must depend on its weakest links – the co-operation of its least co-operative members – for realizing much of its potential in action; that it has on the whole to proceed either by unanimity among its members or by various lopsided voting systems that have been found necessary to reconcile potential members to taking part in its various entities; that there is often a lack of connection between expressed aspiration and action because much relevant action would have costs for significant members who could effectively veto it; that there is a consequent tendency to preoccupation with the formulation of statements of principle and intent; that there is weakness in financial–fiscal arrangements, with members withholding contributions as a form of political pressure or for capricious reasons, so that there is disproportionate prominence of the few entities in the family that are reliably financed agencies (the World Bank Group and the IMF); and that, being an affair of governments, and not the most important arena for many of them, it tends to seem remote from people, even those in politically engaged and informed circles. The family as a whole and its various entities are also convenient as scapegoats for use by governments.

Not all these drawbacks are necessarily irremediable. There have been institutional developments recently that may contain the seeds of improvement. However, there will be no pretence here at proposing general solutions.

What will be suggested are a few further ways in which consensual institutions might come to deal a bit better with some of the key issues for which only governmental union is likely to be ultimately adequate. These are keeping the peace, global environmental security, protecting basic human rights, and combating extreme poverty. An essential fifth, necessary in varying degree for the others, is suitable access to finance. To an extent we are asking consensual institutions to simulate, as far as possible, what a confederal governmental union would be called upon to do.

Some desirable developments in consensual governance

Keeping the peace

Three developments seem important here. One is to extend UN peace-keeping in the direction of what has been called *peace-enforcement*. Under this heading, the introduction of UN troops might still be confined to situations in which there had been a truce between the warring parties, but the forces inserted would aim to be large and strong enough to impose a continuation of peace in case of a serious challenge. Action would be designed to deal with contingencies in which there was less assurance of the goodwill of the parties than has had to be assumed under conventional UN peacekeeping. (Examples might have been Angola after the Lusaka Accord of 1994, or parts of Congo and Sudan more recently.) It might require having national forces that formed a committed standby for UN service, formal UN military staff training, and an enlarged and reliable peacemaking budget. The UN rapid-reaction force proposed by Brian Urquhart and others would probably be designed rather to deal with emergencies, such as cases where there was a clear need recognized for humanitarian intervention without time to wait for a truce or standstill.

A second possibility would be *to recognize, and to define the limits of, justified humanitarian intervention.* There might be both agreed guidelines and an advisory body geared to make prompt recommendations on the subject to the Security Council. After Rwanda and Kosovo, it seems to be widely agreed that there are situations, not necessarily directly threatening interstate warfare, in which intervention, by force if necessary, is needed. As suggested above, the UN might become better equipped to spearhead quick action in these contingencies itself, as well as approving and encouraging the action of states and alliances.

A third possibility is the creation of a *convention and tribunal for dealing with disputes on borders, self-determination, and cultural autonomy.* The disputes covered under these headings would include many of the occasions for warfare, both unofficial and official. States adhering to the convention would undertake to submit disputes in these categories, as defined in the convention, to processes that could entail enquiry, conciliation, and arbitration. There might be a further, more committed, category of members, who would undertake to accept arbitration if all else failed and to comply with any arbitral decisions of the tribunal.

An institution of this general character, depending for its effectiveness on the voluntary consent of governments, is needed *now* under the auspices of the UN. A governmental union developing out of the present EU, which is the main vision of this book, would need a similar convention and tribunal, with all member-states obliged as a condition of their membership to bring disputes of defined character before the tribunal for submission to its processes, and to accept any arbitral decision that it might give. The character of the institution and its purpose would be broadly the same in both cases. If it were already established as a voluntary institution under the UN, then the governmental union descending from the EU might simply make obligatory for all its own member-states the full acceptance of the rules of that convention and tribunal and of its arbitral decisions.

Because of this dual potential, the proposal will be considered more fully below in Chapter 7.

Human rights

Stated simply, the UN might set up arrangements analogous to the European Commission on, and Court of, Human Rights – an investigatory arm, and a tribunal – with a treaty binding governments of states that had adhered to it to accept, and to enforce within their jurisdictions, the rulings of the Court. The Commission and Court would interpret, with respect to particular cases brought before them, the UN conventions on rights. The Court would be a civil one, capable of ordering certain action – on the part of governments and possibly also of corporations or natural persons – to be taken or to cease. This would satisfy a need that is unmet by the machinery, largely empty of teeth, set up to monitor compliance with the UN conventions.

Erskine Childers and Brian Urquhart, in their detailed review of the whole UN system, assert a need 'to establish a judicial resort, an International Human Rights Court, ideally under the World Court' (1994: 111). There is an array of United Nations human rights conventions with procedures for monitoring the observance of the rights that they affirm. At the time of writing there has for a few years been a UN High Commissioner for Human Rights; there have also recently been International Criminal Courts established for ex-Yugoslavia and Rwanda, designed to punish atrocities; and latterly also the creation of an International Criminal Court with more general scope. But, in spite of the value of these institutions and some halting progress, the world's record on human rights is still appalling, and we naturally look for further expedients that may help in piloting a way out.

Paradoxically, there is no world civil court for raising human rights grievances against governments, comparable to the European Court of Human Rights. Under an Optional Protocol (in force from 1976) to the International Covenant on Civil and Political Rights, the UN's Human Rights Committee is empowered to receive complaints from individuals of violations of the Covenant made against states that have become parties to the Protocol. But the states concerned undertake only to reply to such allegations passed on to them by the Committee. By September 2000, 101 states had become parties to the Protocol, but these excluded the USA, China, India, Japan, Indonesia, Pakistan, Bangladesh, Brazil, the United Kingdom, South Africa, and many others of weight. Though its presence no doubt reflects the recognition of a need, the Committee is clearly nothing resembling a court, and apparently much of the world pays not even ritual attention to it.

The possibility of adherence to the treaty proposed here would set a standard of seriousness for dealing with human rights. Adherence could be an object of agitation and lobbying by human rights groups. If the major democratic powers adhered to the treaty, doing so could become a badge of enlightenment and respectability.

Environmental security

The largely successful regime established under the Montreal Protocol of 1987 to preserve the ozone-layer through reduction in CFC and related emissions shows that a purely intergovernmental process may in at least one case deal adequately with a major environmental problem of global scope. But other global-environment challenges may well prove more difficult. In particular, a number of persuasive reasons have been given why solving ozone layer deterioration was intrinsically much easier politically than dealing in a similar way with the control of the greenhouse effect is likely to be. (See Sandler 1997: ch. 4; Barrett 1999.)

Yet the Kyoto Protocol of 1997 does in fact aspire to do an analogous job over precisely that phenomenon of human-generated global warming, a process which is fairly widely agreed to risk drastic changes for large numbers of people, possibly requiring mass displacement and resettlement. That the Protocol was concluded at all amazed some of those familiar with the issues (Grubb et al. 1999). Yet the agreement had from the first manifest weaknesses: it was virtually only the industrialized countries that accepted targets for reducing emissions ('assigned amounts'); the rough principle on which the national targets were based is on equity grounds unlikely ever to have been accepted by most developing countries; though the targets are described as 'legally binding', there is no evident way by which they can be enforced; and in 2001 the largest emitter of all withdrew officially from the agreement. It would seem that both more imagination in the design of the agreement – and above all more commitment, and willingness to make sacrifices, on the part of the major powers – will be needed if a climate-change treaty is to serve its purpose. Even if the agreement as made in 1997 were to be fulfilled as it stood, there are informed doubts over whether its benefits would outweigh its costs.[2] Simulations have suggested that clear net benefit from an agreement on Kyoto lines would at least require the developing countries to accept quotas, and all quotas to be fully tradable among states (Lomborg 2001: 305–12, especially 311). It seems likely that inducing the developing countries to accept quotas must require attention to their natural concerns for equity in the way in which the quotas are fixed. And confidence that the quotas will really guide policy is unlikely unless there is some system of penalties for non-observance that the participating states explicitly accept.

Two possible ways (one of them from Baumert et al.1999; cited Grubb et al. 1999: 263 note) of acceptably meeting the equity requirement, and some of the other requirements, are outlined in Clunies-Ross 2000. It seems quite likely that any comprehensive scheme of quotas or targets, to be acceptable, must involve actual payments from high-income high-emitters to low-income low-emitters. This will have to be accepted, possibly in the form of a system of rewards and penalties for over- and under-compliance – as will, in some form, the full tradability of quotas among states or some close equivalent.

Social justice in the face of world poverty

There are certainly difficulties over making the ideal of social justice 'operational'. However, the world seems to accept in principle that there are certain degrees and manifestations of poverty that must be eliminated – gradually, but with a high priority – and that richer countries have an obligation to contribute officially to this process within the poorer countries in which the poverty is concentrated. All action to this end takes place under strong political constraints. The priority given to it in the rich countries is not always high. In response to an attempt to set operational targets, the world's governments meeting in the UN General Assembly in the year 2000 adopted the 'Millennium Development Goals' (MDGs): eight broad goals, entailing fourteen to eighteen (mostly more specific) 'targets', to be fulfilled by 2015, covering such objectives as halving (from the 1990 level) the proportions of people counted as in poverty and counted as hungry and counted as lacking access to safe drinking water; halting and reversing the spread of AIDS, tuberculosis, and malaria; making complete primary schooling universal for both sexes; and equalizing the proportions of the sexes in secondary, as well as primary, education.

Some very rough estimates have been made of the necessary extra contribution of the rich countries to fulfilling these goals, generally on quite optimistic and demanding assumptions of the additional effort forthcoming from the developing countries. One study from within the World Bank (Devarajan et al. 2002) has produced, from two almost independent processes of reasoning, estimates averaging to $50–60 billion a year for the *additional* Official Development Assistance (ODA) that must be provided by the rich countries – government-to-government or through international bodies – if the MDGs are to be met by 2015. This figure, broadly supported by some other studies, has become accepted. Yet the extra commitments of ODA made in early 2002 – at and soon after the Monterrey Summit, which was intended to put 'financing for development' on a new trajectory – seemed to amount only to about $16 billion a year.

How could the gap be filled? The UK Chancellor of the Exchequer, Gordon Brown, proposed in early 2003 an ingenious device, the International Finance Facility, for using these extra ODA commitments to borrow a much larger annual flow of funds from the financial markets over a limited period leading up to 2015 (UK Treasury and DfID 2003). But there was no sign at the time of writing in mid-2004 that the other industrialized countries, apart from France, would join in this venture; and in any case serious doubts may be raised over whether it is well conceived.

So how might the extra sums needed be raised – both now, to cover the remaining decade of the target period for the MDGs, and hereafter?

Finance

This question is explored in Atkinson 2004, and, more briefly with a different range, in Clunies-Ross 2003. References supporting and explaining what is said here may be found in one or other of these sources.

First – not answering the extra-ODA question, but closely related – international tax co-operation could easily put into the treasuries of developing countries covering a big preponderance of the world's population additional funds at least of the order of $50 billion a year, while at the same time bringing extra revenue, probably much greater in volume, to OECD countries. This is through reducing avoidance and evasion of taxes and also reducing the incentive to reduce tax rates and tax cover for the sake of attracting foreign investment. (See Tanzi 1995 *passim*; Avi-Yonah 2000.) Moves along some of these lines are proceeding haltingly, mainly under the OECD's auspices. Facilitating remittances of emigrant workers to their home countries might also add significantly to the investable resources in the hands of (often quite poor) individuals and households in developing countries.

Second, there is a large potential for private fortunes to make a significant contribution to financing international development, along the lines of the huge sums that have recently come from the Gates Foundation (for medical purposes) and the Turner Foundation. The recent creation of 'Global Funds' (most notably those for AIDS, tuberculosis, and malaria; and for vaccines) – not directly under the institutions of the UN family and permitting a share in their control to go to recipient as well as donor governments, to NGOs, and to private contributors of funds or knowledge – may facilitate more of the really big private contributions.

Third, governments in concert or international organizations might raise funds in ways that obviated or reduced the political difficulties of finding the necessary finance through ordinary budgetary contributions from governments. A number of possibilities are reviewed in Atkinson 2004. Some potentially large examples follow.

1. There might be a globally co-ordinated tax either on some class of transactions unsuitable as a base for independent national taxation, or on some activity that was agreed to have harmful effects whose social costs were not fully reflected in market prices. Some of the suggestions in this latter category are taxes on carbon emissions and on international air transport. A uniform international tax on either of these bases, however, supposes co-ordination, in principle across all the world's governments; and either would raise doubts on the grounds of international equity. Much more satisfactory on both these grounds would be a tax on wholesale currency transactions, which now amount each year to at least $300 trillion. Developments of thought and practice in the late 1990s (Spahn 1996; Schmidt 1999, 2001) showed between them how this tax's use for revenue could be could be pursued independently of any uses that might be made of it for stabilization, and how it

could be collected in a cheap and watertight manner, provided only the monetary authorities of the five 'vehicle-currency' countries would co-operate in imposing it. Its remaining disadvantages are the fanatical opposition it has encountered in the US Congress, and uncertainty about the effect of various rates of tax on the volume of transactions and consequently on the revenue that can be generated. However, much of the opposition is due to misunderstanding and misrepresentation, which may with time be dispelled. And the difficulties due to lack of knowledge on the responsiveness of transactions to rates of tax may be reduced by research, or possibly obviated by starting the tax experimentally at an extremely low rate and gradually raising it. (See Clunies-Ross 2003.) Grounds have been advanced for thinking that a currency tax at 0.02 per cent would have little effect on the volume of transactions and therefore might on its own raise revenue of the order of $50–55 billion a year (Spahn 2002).

2. A further possibility is the direct use of a power of credit-creation that has been given to an international institution. This is the IMF's power of issuing Special Drawing Rights (SDRs) to its members, normally in proportion to their IMF quotas, a power that has not been used since 1981. Its use was blocked by the governments of four major economic powers until the mid-1990s. Thereafter, when the US administration was willing, in the mid-1990s, and a proposal to issue SDRs gained sufficient support from the representatives of other governments in the IMF, the issue of SDRs was blocked by the US Congress – but the Congress's power to do so depended on special circumstances that will not necessarily recur. Recently two very senior IMF insiders (Clark and Polak 2002) and also the Zedillo High-Level Panel (UN 2001: 58–9) have pointed out the real-income and stabilization benefits to most developing countries that would result from regular SDR allocations. In addition, Soros (2002) has argued for an agreement under which rich countries would surrender their allocations of SDRs to be used for world-development purposes – something that IMF rules would permit (Boughton 2001: 933). These allocations would be of little or no value to most rich countries because those countries' authorities could raise funds in the markets at similar costs to the interest they would have to pay on their allocations of SDRs. (By contrast, most developing countries would need to pay higher rates of interest if they were to borrow in the markets.) On common estimates of what size of annual SDR allocation could be absorbed (say, $30–35 billion), this might allow SDRs valued at around $12–20 billion to

be diverted for development each year. It seems inevitable, however, given the features of SDRs, that these sums would be available not as grants but as low-interest termless loans (see Clunies-Ross 2003). These might still have important development and welfare uses, for example to reduce the burden of those debts of developing-country governments that involved higher servicing costs; as low-cost sources of finance for productive investment; or as costless ways for global-development institutions to hold reserves.

★★★

Altogether, there are a number of ways in which consensual global institutions might be further developed to serve better those functions of governance for which we have argued that a governmental union is ultimately necessary.

Summary of Chapter 5

- The long-term aim of achieving a world governmental union of confederal character – for the purpose of keeping the peace, environmental security, protecting human rights, and fulfilling the rudimentary demands of social justice by reducing extreme poverty – need in no way conflict with the use and development of consensual international institutions for pursuing the same ends in the present.

- Several expedients are suggested here for increasing the scope and effectiveness of the consensual arrangements available through the UN family and related institutions in their tasks of keeping the peace, protecting human rights, and achieving environmental security. But some of these approaches entail additional financial costs, as clearly also does the pursuit of the world community's currently accepted objectives for reducing the extremes of poverty.

- Estimates are cited of the additional annual sums required from international sources, over and above the extra likely to be generated within the countries directly concerned, for fulfilling the Millennium Development Goals – in such fields as health, education, water-supply, and sanitation – by the year 2015.

• These sums are roughly of the order of the amounts of annual Official Development Assistance presently provided by the high-income countries; their provision therefore requires something like a doubling of that effort. This additional finance from international sources needed on these estimates to fulfil the Millennium Development Goals would amount to between an additional 0.2 per cent and 0.3 per cent of the affluent countries' aggregate incomes, and in principle it could be provided through national appropriations according to an agreed scale. But proposals are in the air and cited here through which the finance might be made available in ways that are politically less difficult or painful.

Notes

1. 'The UN family' is taken to include the United Nations Organization (General Assembly and its Committees, Security Council, Secretariat), the Specialized Agencies (World Health Organization, Food and Agriculture Organization, International Labour Organization, and the many others), the Bretton Woods Institutions (World Bank Group and International Monetary Fund), and the World Trade Organization.

2. The doubts admittedly tend to ignore the less 'automatic' impacts of the commitments, for example in stimulating research and consequent changes in relative costs. See, for example, Grubb 2000.

Chapter 6

Constitutional features of a global confederation

The details of a constitution can be important. No constitution can be a guarantee against disaster. There will need to be implicit rules observed, beside those that are written or otherwise explicit. But it is all too easy to frame provisions that do not take account of how politicians and electorates behave, or specifically of how they are likely to behave in the circumstances for which the particular constitution is designed. The positive suggestions made in this chapter cannot pretend to represent the only satisfactory, or necessarily the best, answer. They are merely an attempt to think past possible hazards, some of which will be peculiar to the very wide and diverse confederation contemplated. They aim to show that there is at least one model of constitution that has some prospect of being both acceptable and workable.

Unless its constitution quells the fears of those that would have to consent to join it, a confederation will never be formed. On the other hand, unless it is likely to permit action on a number of issues, it will not be worth forming. The constitution will have to steer a course between too many checks and too few. A solution must rest on finding *the right kind and pattern of checks*.

General principles and particular constraints

To be attractive to the various constituencies whose agreement it would have to secure, the confederation we are considering would need to be clearly limited constitutionally, with safeguards against its encroachment on the usual personal freedoms of liberal societies or, without clear signalling and widespread consent, on the powers that have initially been agreed to remain with the component states. It would need to be democratic in form, with orderly procedures for change of government. But there might also need to be other safeguards to stem anxieties that could be widespread within certain of the component states.

Some account will be taken here of the fact that the core of a global or near-global association is supposed to develop out of the framework of the European Union, which has a history and constitution of its own. This background will probably make some solutions easier to reach, and on that ground more eligible, than others that in the abstract may seem as good or better. An Appendix to the chapter considers how the proposals presented by the Convention on the Future of Europe in June–July 2003, and amended by the Inter-Governmental Conference to give in June 2004 the Draft Treaty establishing a Constitution for Europe (European Union 2004), seem likely to further, or to hinder, the role of the Union envisaged here.

There follow some of the questions that the framers of a constitution for a democratic federation or confederation would have to answer.

Representation by governments or people?

In our definitions in Chapter 3, we specified that a consensual union would be directed entirely by its member-governments, unanimously or not, but left it open whether a governmental union might also be controlled by member-governments or must necessarily have some other form of driver.

So far, then, as our argument has gone to this point, the major organs dispensing the confederation's powers might be *either* elected by the people of the countries making it up *or* composed of the representatives of governments. All modern federations lean heavily to the former model, even though some have upper chambers representative of state governments (Germany) or of state parliaments together with other constituencies (India). In fact there may well be doubts whether a union governed entirely by representatives of component-state governments (even well before the union had become universal) *could* operate as a governmental union with the attributes that this book supposes are needed: one able to act consistently and coherently as a government possessing great responsibilities – including those of foreign policy and defence. Probably a multinational authority that is in the hands of delegates of state governments – even if it is empowered to act, say, by simple majority of those delegates – could not be expected to constitute a workable government, one that might deliver effective autonomy to the whole.

The present European Union is a mixture: it started with most of the decisive formal power in the hands of the delegates of governments in the Council (though with the distinctive complication of giving much initiative and control over detail to the government-nominated Commission, whose members, once appointed, are intended to be independent of the governments that have selected them), but it then shifted gradually to give increasing (though not yet fully co-equal) authority to directly elected representatives in the Parliament.

It will be assumed here that the hypothetical world confederation will be constituted mainly on the popular principle: the main house of its legislature directly elected by the people, with individual electors' votes of roughly uniform weight.

For the whole world, on existing populations, it is possible to imagine a parliament consisting, for example, of one representative from each country together with an extra one for each complete ten million people. This would entail a parliament of roughly 800 members: large but not inordinately so – slightly larger than the present European Parliament, which, with the cap of 736 proposed in the 2004 draft Constitution (Article I-19(2)), would itself be not much larger than the British House of Commons. In relation to population this distribution of seats would underweight the really large states by about 25 per cent, and of course greatly overweight the smallest states, but that would probably fall within the limits of acceptance.

The principle of (almost) uniform weighting of votes would of course make it absolutely essential that free elections should be guaranteed; the potential members could not be allowed to join unless that condition would be manifestly fulfilled. Any suspicion that the franchises of say a fifth of the parliament might be controlled by a single authoritarian government would not be tolerable. Aspiring members would not be admitted unless it seemed as certain as these things can be that elections on their territory would be free within a context of substantially free expression and debate. This is of course an implication of the present conditions of entry to the EU.

One big reason why the alternative (of representation by governments) would be less satisfactory – and possibly unworkable in a confederal government required to have an active executive role – is that it would tend to identify each issue of contention as one in which any given state was either for or against, and hence each outcome as one in which that state was either a winner or a loser. All political battles would therefore tend to become (often quite artificially) issues between states. Election by the people, on the other hand, allows a diversity of views, parties, factions, to emerge among the representatives of each country, leading inevitably to alliances that cut across state boundaries. A defeat on an issue is not therefore necessarily a defeat for certain countries. Similarly (on the assumption that the executive is chosen by the legislature), the executive would be much less likely to find itself opposed in effect by certain countries if the legislature were constituted by direct popular election rather than by governments. The existing federations, whose parliaments or predominant lower chambers are chosen by popular election, have given no reason for supposing that they would work better if they consisted of representatives of the governments of their component states.

But for the present purpose there is a qualifier. Though 'upper' (in the modern British sense of secondary) legislative chambers are not in general very useful, there may, in the case we are considering – a diverse and multinational confederation – be a constructive role for a legislative body representing governments as a corrective in certain circumstances to the popularly elected chamber. This question will be considered below.

Checks on the majority

A confederal constitution that can be changed but not too easily, entrenched individual rights of various sorts, and courts to interpret these provisions: all this goes without saying. There is also much to be said for explicitly leaving some powers in the hands of component states (with possibly also some wider enforceable guarantees of subsidiarity). But a confederation covering all or much of the world, with the areas of jurisdiction contemplated here, would probably need a further kind of check on the power of the majority if it were ever to come into being.

A world confederal parliament elected roughly in proportion to population would represent predominantly poor people and poor countries. Even if the distribution of income across the world altered considerably from its current pattern, it is still extremely likely that many more than half the people would earn below world-average income. This is implied by a so-called 'positively skewed' income distribution, which is strongly marked within most or all countries as well as across the world population of today. On the World Bank's 1998 figures (World Bank 2000: 231), low-income countries alone made up 60 per cent of the world's population (and just 20 per cent of its income at purchasing-power parity, or only 6.4 per cent of income on exchange-rate comparisons), and low-income and middle-income countries together 85 per cent of people (and 43 per cent of income on purchasing-power comparisons or 22 per cent at exchange rates).

Issues of redistribution (through taxes, transfers, and spending) will inevitably be extremely important in a confederation such as we are supposing. With equal weighting of individual votes, the present high-income countries, extremely rich by world standards, would have on 1998 figures 15 per cent of the voting power and 57 per cent of the income (or as much as 78 per cent of the income on conventional exchange-rate comparisons). What might seem to the poor majority a modest redistribution of spending power could well look to the rich minority like merciless plunder. With 85 per cent of the voting power and no further checks, the representatives of the low- and middle-income countries could, on ostensibly quite fair principles, transfer to the use of their populations considerable resources from the high-income countries. It is possible to envisage transfers of this sort which would be seen as destructive by the peoples of the rich countries and would in prospect be completely unacceptable to them.

It is true that the widespread fears among the propertied classes of the past that democracy would lead to uninhibited equalizations of wealth have been very far from fulfilment. Yet a constitution that has any prospect of allowing redistribution without limit will simply not be acceptable to those high-income countries. It is also pretty clear that some of the checks on popular majorities that have been applied – generally for different reasons – in other federal and confederal systems will not by themselves serve adequately for this purpose: the equal representation by states in the US and Australian Senates, for example; representation of state governments or legislatures in federal upper chambers, as in Germany and India. Quite apart from the fact that upper chambers in the British tradition often have no power over money measures, these devices would fail to provide reliably the safeguard required, and at the same time quite possibly lead to unnecessary obstruction and immobility. To be suitable, a provision would need to be tailored to the need.

There is, however, a fairly simple solution capable of addressing the problem directly and in a way that is transparently clear. This is to require money bills in the confederal parliament – and decisions on certain other crucial matters, including the election or endorsement of a new Executive – to achieve at least passive consent from no less than a certain proportion of members in each 'house', where house does not mean a legislative chamber in the usual sense but rather the members in the main ('lower') legislative chamber representing the countries of a self-selected group. (To avoid confusion, some other term could be used: order, phalanx, phylum, moiety, clan, corps.)

The constitution might require, say, a three-quarters majority in any house to vote against a measure in one of the relevant classes for the veto to be exercised. It would after all be reasonable to require that the people of a group of countries should be very firmly against a measure before this check on the majority was allowed to bite.

There would need to be a lower limit on the population of the countries covered by a house, say half a billion or a billion people, and, subject to that constraint, the houses could be self-selecting. The larger the number of houses, potentially the more difficult it would be to get any budgetary measure or other vetoable decision approved. But the minimum number of people permitted to be covered by each would have to be set low enough to reassure the groups that might think it necessary to protect themselves against an overall majority. Such groups might include not just the affluent countries but also perhaps (say) sub-Saharan Africa or Latin America or the poor primary-exporters. A lower limit of 0.8 billion on 1998 figures would be low enough to allow the affluent OECD countries to act as a house, but the critical number would need to go down to about 0.6 billion if it were to accommodate sub-Saharan Africa as a complete house, and this would permit a theoretical maximum of eight houses on present populations (given that India and China could constitute no more than one house each). There would be an inevitable trade-off between reassurance and the risk of immobility.

If world confederation is to come about mainly through development and extension of the institutions of the European Union and its relatives, which we have argued is the most promising route, then it would seem important, at some point in the Union's expansion, to institute this safeguard as a constitutional device that could be invoked. Actually to implement it – before it was needed as a precondition for making a particular enlargement acceptable – might be courting difficulties. But it would need to be kept in the negotiators' armoury. Its presence would by no means preclude substantial redistribution of resources from richer to poorer. It would merely give the rich, and other large groups of nations with perceived interests in common – once they had taken account of all moral and political pressures brought to bear by the other elements in the system – the ultimate opportunity to say 'thus far and no further'.

Provisions against deadlock

To avoid immobility in the face of a veto power over a new Executive or a budget, there should be a provision prolonging the tenure of the previous Executive, and prolonging budgetary appropriations until replacements (an Executive or a budget) had been duly approved. The EU has a system called 'provisional twelfths' for prolonging budgetary authorization month by month when there has been a delay in approval of a new budget (Bainbridge 2002: 34). Its draft Constitution would continue this.

Washington, Westminster, Paris, or Bern?

Which form of constitutional democracy would suit the case best: one in which the chief executive is directly and personally elected for a fixed term quite separately from the legislature; one in which the executive is effectively appointed by, and responsible to, the legislature and therefore has to depend for its continued existence on the support of a majority of parliamentarians; a compromise between these two, in which executive power is divided between a directly elected fixed-term president and a parliamentarily responsible (and dismissible) cabinet; or the much rarer Swiss version, under which the executive is appointed by the legislature, subject to certain rules (purely customary in the Swiss case, but not necessarily so) designed to keep it representative of the various main strands in the population (political, linguistic, and communal), and remains in place for a fixed term until a new parliamentary election?

The Swiss model depends on a longstanding habit of consensus forged to deal with particular sources of potential division. There may be good reasons why it is a unique bird. The Washington pattern ensures that there is always an executive but does not guarantee co-operation between executive and legislature. Westminster provides a fair prospect of co-operation between the two arms whenever an executive is securely in place, but, in the absence of a small number of well-organized parties, runs the risk that there will be transient executives or even at times none at all. In comparison with Washington, it favours strong party organization in the parliament and a corresponding emphasis on common 'union', as against local, issues. The Paris (Gaullist) version is a halfway house between these two without obviously reaping the advantages or avoiding the drawbacks of either. Shorn of its special customary rules about the composition of the executive, the Swiss model might also be regarded as a compromise between Westminster and Washington, with a government chosen by the legislature but guaranteed a fixed term.

Washington in its standard form depends on the popular election of a single person to head, and in fact to be, the executive. Once elected, the person has unique authority to initiate executive action, though her or his capacity to carry it out is limited by the legislature and by the courts. For the world, or a large part of it, this might be putting too many eggs into one basket. Even if the roulette of a first-past-the-post system of voting were ruled out, the selection of one person for a fixed term would surely be thought just too risky. Someone with appeal across the world (or less unappealing than all others) might be a moral leader with political nous (a Mandela or a Havel or an M. K. Gandhi, if any more of these species existed), but might also be an aspiring tyrant or an incompetent over policy or power-dealing or both.

He or she might be dangerously free of the salutary shackles of a widely based cross-border party or alliance of parties as selector and power-base. A variant in which a three-person or even larger executive was chosen directly by single transferable vote might be safer but still perhaps not safe enough. The French compromise, in which the directly elected president has only some of the executive functions, carries some of the same risks, their severity depending on which functions exactly are involved.

The Westminster model, in which the executive is chosen by the local delegates – for, among other attributes, a capacity for getting along with at least a majority from among them – seems a safer starting-point, especially because it means that the executive may be changed by the legislature. In their readiness to accept various forms of constitution, people will probably lean to the side of caution about any possibility of concentration of power. At the same time, because of the risk of instability in political allegiances and hence of frequent losses of confidence in the executive, use would need to be made of simple devices for ensuring that there would always be an executive and there would always be a budget: the legislators might, for example, as suggested above, be left with the existing team and an extension of the existing financial authorization until they could agree on replacements. One possible option is that the executive, once chosen by the legislature, would be installed for a fixed term, as in Switzerland; but this would negate what may well be a major reassuring feature of the Westminster system: the ready removability of the executive. Possibly the best compromise, then, is to make the executive removable by the legislature if and when a stipulated majority of the legislators can agree on a replacement.

The arrangement mooted above for a veto by 'houses', combined with provisions against deadlock, enhances the case for a Westminster-type system, in that it provides some safeguards against both elective tyranny and the form of immobility to which such a system can be subject.

A role for an upper chamber representing governments

Proceeding from the European Union as it is, we find ourselves endowed with the equivalent of a chamber representing governments: the Council of Ministers and European Council, which for this purpose may be considered as a single entity ('the Council'). This body has considerable power within the Union, and we may well surmise that governments will be unwilling to relinquish that power entirely. So we may explore the question whether the Council might still have a potentially useful function in the structure that is being foreshadowed here: one in which the directly and more or less proportionally elected chamber has the dominant position that it usually occupies in Westminster-style democracies.

For the two key matters of finance and the nomination of the executive, we have supposed that each 'house' in the lower chamber, voting by a suitable large majority, may exercise a veto on change. Assume those provisions are in place. Perhaps what is further needed from a chamber representing governments is a power *in extremis* of facilitating as well as one of obstructing.

Where both chambers are party-dominated – as is common in Europe, Japan, and Australasia – a revising upper chamber, whether nominated by state governments or parliaments or alternatively directly elected on a different system or timetable, tends to rubber-stamp when it is dominated by the same party as the lower chamber and to obstruct in the opposite case. Whether or not it blocks or significantly modifies bills often depends more on accidents of electoral timing than on the merits of the case. Any tendency of a dominant party in the lower chamber, or the executive that it endorses, to act tyrannically from the viewpoint of a minority in that chamber will hence not be reliably resisted by the usual Westminster-model upper chamber.

However, in the situation we are supposing – a wide international confederation – ideology-based or class-based party is likely to matter less, even within a popularly elected chamber, than in the familiar exemplars of the Westminster model; and country, region, economic structure, average income level, or religious tradition, correspondingly more. The form of elective tyranny of most concern is likely to be the perceived oppression of countries with certain common features by others that happen to have the numbers. It is against this type of feared or imagined abuse that the house-veto device suggested above is directed.

But the present European Parliament, and any successors covering even wider spheres, may be relatively weak in a feature generally characteristic of elective chambers of parliaments in the Westminster tradition. This is the discipline that comes from a government's power of patronage. A party in office has ministerial posts to distribute to some of its supporters in parliament, often to quite a large proportion of them. Where an executive is chosen other than from within the parliament, this lever of legitimate patronage as a way of generating some discipline behind a governing party's position is absent. The EU's Commission, at present and also under the 2004 draft Constitution, is chosen under procedures that do not associate it with membership of the Parliament or adherence to a dominant party or alliance in the Parliament. Even if that were altered, so that the President of the Commission came to be elected by the Parliament alone from among its members, and the other members of the Commission or Executive were chosen by her or him from members of the Parliament, the number of members of the Commission might be so small in relation to those of the Parliament that the leverage thereby given to the Executive would be weak. With weak party discipline, the Executive might have to bargain with individual members for their support. Lacking the weapon of appointment patronage, the Executive could come to rely on 'pork': the favouring – often inefficient and inequitable – of particular constituencies. Moreover, the lack of party discipline might lead to irresponsible censure and dismissal motions on the Executive. In an attempt to reap the benefits of a Westminster system, we might find ourselves saddled with the failings of Washington but without its principal bonus.

The proposed house-veto, necessary though it might be, would tend to aggravate these failings. A three-quarters majority say in one 'house', representing less than a tenth perhaps of the total elected chamber, could block a budget that a large overall majority was prepared to accept, and this might be out of sheer irresponsibility or as a way of bargaining for some partial benefits to the region involved. Or – on the supposition that a house-veto could be applied to the appointment of a new Commission President or Chief Executive – a large segment of one house, from the same motives, might block the appointment, and so keep in being an Executive that had genuinely and justly lost the confidence of the parliamentary majority.

As an expedient that would be unlikely to neutralize the intended function of the house-veto but might sometimes block its abuse, a second chamber representing governments – the continuation of the Council – might be permitted, by a particularly large majority (say of votes of governments representing 95 per cent or 90 per cent of the Union's population, the figure determined with reference to the minimum population of the countries represented by a 'house'), to respond to an appeal from the majority in the directly elected chamber to override a house-veto. Probably good rather than harm overall would also result from allowing the Council, but only by a similarly large majority, to amend or nullify conclusively any non-financial bill from the other chamber. And, by its usual ('qualified') majority (say, the 55 per cent of states and 65 per cent of population proposed in the draft Constitution), it might be permitted to return any such bill for reconsideration.

At present in the EU, the Council (European Council and Council of Ministers) has a much greater relative role within the system than this suggests. It may be that governments will be unwilling to see the Council's role reduced. So we may have to look for a compromise with current arrangements rather than the ideal. The position as proposed in the draft Constitution will be discussed in the Appendix to this chapter.

A constitutional umpire

A federal or confederal constitution requires courts to interpret the division of powers between the various governments. Westminster-style political systems generally also have a non-executive head of state whose main political function is to authorize the transfer of power from one executive or one parliament to another. This umpire might, as suggested below, be chosen by an upper chamber representing the governments, the successor to the Council, or by some other method. It might be the Council as a body. But it is important that the person or body fulfilling the role should not, unless in highly exceptional circumstances, be dismissable by any of the entities over whose tenure of power she or he or it has to make decisions. The draft Constitution's proposals (Article I-21) might be taken to point to the possibility that the new-style President of the European Council should play this role if, as envisaged here, the Commission were to develop into a regular Executive.

The right to secede

The term 'confederation' has been used here to imply a right to secede. The terms on which secession could take place should probably be formalized by the constitution. The draft EU Constitution (Article I-59) makes the terms of secession a matter of negotiated agreement between the seceder and the Union, with secession occurring two years after the seceder has notified its intention if by then no agreement has been reached. But, if there were a more developed union, with military plant and equipment involved, more defined rules might be necessary.

Though depending entirely on the people of the country for which secession was contemplated, a decision to secede should not be made so easy as to risk happening on a whim or the proverbial fit of absence of mind. For example, secession might be taken to require two enhanced majorities, with an interval between them of say one to three years, of the electors in the state for which secession was proposed, on a motion backed by a majority of the Union's parliamentary members representing the people of that state. It would be best if the state government could be kept out of the initiating process for secession in order to reduce the risk that secession might come about through a power competition between authorities rather than because of strong popular feeling.

Guidelines should be laid down on the share of the net assets or liabilities of the confederation a seceding member should take over, with arbitration in case of dispute; but it would probably need to be made clear that there would be no recognized claim on the seceding member's part to any share of actual military equipment of the union or to control or ownership of any union military installation that happened to be on its territory. In fact, settlement over military matters in case of secession would probably be the most difficult area with the kind of confederation we are considering. If the understanding on which states have joined the union is that they intend to remain within it except in extreme circumstances, then it is appropriate that secession should carry some cost for the seceder. Those who remained in the union would also want to be assured that the sharing-out of military installations and hardware and intelligence would not result in equipping a seceding former member to attack or threaten the remainder of the union more effectively than if it had never joined. On both scores, guidelines that veered towards toughness on the seceder would probably be needed on division of the military durables, with an arbitration procedure over the details.

Constitutional implications for the EU

If the European Parliament is to serve as the germ of the principal chamber of a world confederal parliament, it could usefully move – at least over the few fields represented here as crucial for central author-ity – toward exercising the powers, as against other constitutional ele-ments (the Council and Commission), that a 'true' and much wider confederation seems likely to need in its elected legislative chamber. This is the direction in which it has in fact slowly moved and one that seems likely to continue. Proposals fairly recently mooted at the time of writing (the first of them accepted, the second advanced in some degree, in the draft Constitution) would have a Council President selected by the European Council (representing the governments) to hold office for a significant period, and the President of the Commission elected by the Parliament. These could be appropriate next steps. Thereafter gradually the Commission might be turned into a more conventional Executive, eventually selected entirely by the President of the Commission in her or his capacity as the Parliament's choice for Chief Executive, though possibly subject as a whole to approval by the Parliament; while the Council, as mooted above, might become increasingly like a revising or delaying legislative upper chamber, and its President might possibly become the day-to-day umpire over transfer of power from one executive to another and one elected chamber to another: the equivalent of a non-executive head of state. The draft Constitution's proposed moves in these areas are considered in the Appendix to this chapter.

If the franchises in the Parliament were roughly in proportion to population (modified solely by a rule that each state should have at least one member), then in the Council something like the distribution of votes used hitherto for qualified-majority purposes, under which smaller states are more highly represented in relation to population than larger ones, might be considered tolerable. But much better than past ways of doing this – because simple and rational and robust to changing membership – is the definition of a Council qualified majority proposed in the draft Constitution: the assent of members representing at least 55 per cent of states and at least 65 per cent of the population of the Union. Equal representation of all states, as in the US and Australian upper chambers, would be clearly inappropriate in a legislative chamber potentially representing entities from China to Nauru, one with about 100,000 times as many people as the other, or even from Germany to Luxembourg, Cyprus, and Malta. But some fairly marked bias, at least in blocking power, toward smaller states, such as the rule proposed in the draft Constitution would entail, might be permanently acceptable if the upper chamber were to be essentially a revising and delaying body without power on money matters or on the identity of the executive, and its threshold majority for changing or delaying decisions of the elected chamber were set fairly high.

In any case, it would be important, as soon as possible, to arrive at some coherent and sustainable rules for allocating votes in the Council and for determining the number of members from each state in the Parliament, so that these would not have to be renegotiated with each new accession of members. The draft Constitution's proposal would deal neatly with the first of these requirements. A similarly robust formula for determining the number of members from each state in the Parliament could be developed by modifying, simplifying, and generalizing the agreements made in the Treaty of Nice to deal with the 2004 enlargement. The draft Constitution's provision in Article I-19(2) does not seem precise enough to give a unique answer at each point in the Union's growth.

Upper chambers in Westminster-type systems are notable mostly for nuisance value and for giving scope to party games. Arguably they are best when they have least real power – like the British House of

Lords, which if resisted can merely revise (revocably) and delay, and then only non-financial legislation, allowing for second thoughts on the part of the dominant lower chamber. Nevertheless, the member-state governments will doubtless be unwilling to bow out entirely, and, as suggested above, keeping the Council as a modest revising chamber, with certain last-ditch powers for extreme circumstances, could be a tolerable and even useful compromise.

Coping with variable geometry

In Chapter 4 it was argued that a measure of 'variable geometry' should be positively embraced by the European movement. In other words it should not be considered objectionable that two or more states might be united on some issues and not on others. This is quite simply necessary if the existing European Union is to provide the kernel of a world confederation. It is also in fact how the European movement, even in some measure the EU itself, has worked hitherto.

The aim should be to have a 'core' of Union powers to which all members would be subject, covering the key areas in which overriding global decisions are needed: defence (which implies many elements of foreign policy while the union is incomplete), human rights, and environmental issues of global or trans-state-border scope. It should also have financial powers sufficient to allow it to implement policy in these areas and also to provide the resources for reducing extreme poverty and social injustice. Because of the history and dynamics of the European movement, it has also to cover and administer an area of free trade and free capital movement, though it would be best perhaps if there were plenty of provision for temporary blocks and transitional arrangements.

But subgroups of Union member-states will want to unite in other fields, such as over a common currency and over a single labour market and immigration policy and open internal borders. At present these latter unions are supposed and designed to be universal within the EU; but in fact the common currency so far is not; the single labour market is in practice less than complete; some borders within the Union are still controlled; and there is no realization yet of a common immigration policy, without which completely free internal labour movement can hardly be sustainable. On the other hand, under articles added (by the 1997 Treaty of Amsterdam) to the Maastricht Treaty and the

Treaty of Rome, closer co-operation among members on matters not covered by the treaties, but making use 'of the institutions, procedures and mechanisms' set out in these two treaties, is permitted only on restrictive conditions, so restrictive in fact that some regard that sort of co-operation as virtually excluded (Bainbridge 2002: 283).

My argument would be for a reversal of these presumptions, as the draft Constitution probably goes some way towards doing in its Articles on 'Enhanced Co-operation' (Articles I-43, III-322 to III-329). Where individual members already regard themselves as having powerful reasons for remaining outside certain less essential aspects of union, or where it seems likely that an insistence on universal membership for purposes of these elements of union would render a much wider union on the most vital matters impossible, such areas of openness or uniformity, though they may be potentially desirable in themselves and be desired jointly by significant numbers of members, should be regarded as optional extras, eligible to be administered through the machinery of the Union where that is practicable, and not frowned on but welcomed. This approach is likely to run up against a passion for neatness and uniformity. But these essentially aesthetic considerations should surely be given a much lower priority than the long-term aspiration to world peace, security, and justice – which an excessive concern for tidiness may obstruct.

It would be nice if everyone could travel and work freely everywhere and if the same money were acceptable from Novaya Zemlya to Cape Horn. But there are sufficient and unavoidable reasons in the world as it is, and as it is likely to be over the coming half-century, why that cannot be, or on good grounds will not be. This should not stop us from opening borders and sharing currencies as widely as we can without hazarding other important objectives. It is hard to see how the peoples within the border-post-free Schengen area thereby harm those (the Irish and British) outside it or vice versa. It is also hard to see how the decision on the part of the Danes, Swedes, and British not to join the euro – or the decision of the other twelve of the pre-2004 fifteen to join it – is an injury or affront to the other group in either case. Neither the ins nor the outs for either of these unions can be regarded as free-riding on the rest. There is no obvious reason why any state should join a union of this kind, or refrain from joining one, if it foresees more harm than gain to its people from doing so. There is no clear common good that a minority of states that choose either to be in or to be out while the majority choose otherwise are impairing. Conversely, to admit an applicant to the Union, while refusing to admit it to one of these optional extra associations on the ground that it does not meet the agreed conditions that that optional extra must impose, is not necessarily monstrous or unfair. (This is in fact what happens at present over the euro: until the Maastricht tests are satisfied, the new member may not take part in 'Economic and Monetary Union'.)

There are also perfectly manageable ways of dealing politically and administratively with at least some of these optional extras through extensions of the Union's machinery. For example, only those members of the Parliament and of the Council representing countries covered by an agreement to run a particular activity in common should vote when decisions have to be made about it. Where the activity would otherwise fall under the Commission (which might have matured into the Executive), a Commissioner (or Minister) should be appointed *ad hoc* by the relevant subgroup of members in the appropriate institution (members of the Parliament, or perhaps of the Council if appointment is still in the hands of governments), independently of the then-current arrangements for appointing the rest of the Commission or Executive. How far the 'core' and the 'optional' Commissioners should be bound to act together would be a matter for decision. Any additional funding necessary would have to be raised by a union-tax surcharge on the countries concerned. Alternatively, there could simply be separate unions for optional matters. If these imitated the constitution of the core Union, the two solutions could be identical in effect.

The draft Constitution, though cautious, has, in its Articles on 'Enhanced Co-operation', proposed sensible arrangements for extending the machinery of the Union to cover certain agreements to act in common made by a third or more of the member-states. Its proposed Article I-29 also accepts explicitly that some member-states will not be using the euro and adapts governing arrangements accordingly.

These arrangements for what are in effect overlapping unions on particular subjects may at first sight seem anomalous, but are probably no more so than some of those that have already worked or been projected in the Union. Examples were the two new 'pillars' (Common Foreign and Security Policy, and Justice and Home Affairs) introduced by the Maastricht Treaty, with in each case less power and responsibility given to the Commission and to the Parliament than over other activities of the Union: there has, since 1999, been a High Representative for the Common Foreign and Security Policy appointed by the European Council (Bainbridge 2002: 319–20), while the Commission has also had a member with a foreign-affairs portfolio. The European Central Bank too operates independently of the Commission, and its Board is appointed by a process involving the member governments, their central-bank governors, and the Parliament (Bainbridge 2002: 189). The European movement has been expert at accepting sensible anomalies.

Those of us who wished to do so could have a common or almost-common European currency and a common or almost-common European area of labour movement (and Europe for these purposes could cover any country that accepted the necessary responsibilities and was accepted by the other members) – while at the same time still flexibly using in the service of the world this unique governmental instrument that has emerged over the past half-century.

Summary of Chapter 6

- A democratic confederal constitution would have to steer a course between on the one hand having inadequate safeguards against the tyranny of the majority, and on the other hand having so many checks that it ran a high risk of immobility.

- The constitution should limit central powers, safeguard personal immunities, and provide orderly and democratic procedures for changes of government and for its own amendment, with courts to interpret its application.

- Representation in the sole or predominant legislative chamber should be of the people of the area covered, roughly in proportion to their numbers, rather than of the governments of the component states.

- In the special conditions of a global or near-global, or at least widely diverse, confederation, there need to be means by which representatives of sufficiently large self-selected groups of countries may (provided a large majority of them is in favour of doing so) veto new measures in certain particularly sensitive fields, probably money measures and selection of a new executive. To prevent inertia from resulting, an existing executive could remain in power, and relevant existing financial provisions remain in force, or be automatically extended, until replaced.

- With these safeguards against elective tyranny on the one hand and partisan obstruction on the other, it seems that a Westminster-type system, with the executive responsible to the legislature, would be preferable to any of the main alternatives.

- Yet, because, in the circumstances likely to prevail, a government's hold through patronage over a section of the legislature is likely to be weak, it may be useful to retain a chamber representing governments, descended from the present Council of Ministers and European Council, with certain last-ditch powers (exercised only by very large majorities) to counteract irresponsibility in the elected chamber, especially if the provisions mooted for veto powers to subgroups of members in the latter are implemented.

- As characteristically in Westminster-type systems, there probably needs to be a constitutional umpire playing the role of a non-executive head of state, who has certain supervisory functions over changes of legislature and executive and is not removable by any of the entities over whose tenure she or he has to pronounce.

- There should be a right of secession for the people of any member-state, under procedures laid down in the constitution and designed both to prevent over-hasty decisions and also to avoid giving a seceding member any military advantage from having entered and left the confederation.

- In order to move toward a structure of this sort, existing EU institutions could be modified to have a medium-term President of the European Council elected by that Council (as recently agreed by the Inter-Governmental Conference), and to have the President of the Commission elected by the European Parliament. The President of the Commission could then gradually assume the role of a more conventional Chief Executive and be given authority (alone or subject to parliamentary approval) to choose the other members of the Commission, which would become more like a Westminster-style executive, responsible to the Parliament. The Council might, with a simplified voting structure, become a revising and delaying upper chamber, without power in normal circumstances over money matters or the composition of the Executive, but possibly with certain overriding authority that could be wielded, given a very large measure of agreement among its members, in extraordinary circumstances. The successor to the President of the European Council might fulfil the role of a non-executive head of state.

• To manage 'variable geometry' – the fact that subgroups of members of the Union (with non-members possibly also participating) wish to unite in the governance of some field of activity in which joint action cannot acceptably be made universal within the Union – it may be possible, in one of the sensible 'anomalies' at which the EU is adept, to have only certain members of the Parliament and of the Council (those from the countries participating in co-operation over that field of governance), voting over matters in which not all members participate, and to have an extraordinary member of the Commission or Executive appointed by the Parliament's members (or the Council's members) from the participating countries in order to manage the field of governmental activity concerned.

Appendix

Implications of the 'Draft Treaty Establishing a Constitution for Europe' presented in June 2004 by the Conference of the Representatives of the Governments of the Member States

At the time of going to press in the northern autumn of 2004, the proposals made by the Convention on the Future of Europe in the previous year had been adopted with some amendments by an Inter-Governmental Conference in mid-June. The draft Constitution was then to be subject to ratification by the twenty-five national parliaments, and in a number of cases also to popular referendum. So we should still be dealing, at the end of 2004 and possibly for a year or more later, with ideas that were on the table but some way short of being endorsed. The proposals considered here may have to go through further revisions or even lapse entirely. This review of the proposals' implications for the hopes expressed in this book deals only with items of major interest to our argument. It makes use of *The Economist*'s summaries of the Convention's report (21.6.2003: 23–5) and of the draft Constitution (26.6.2004: 42); draws on the European Parliament delegation's summary of the draft Constitution; and refers to the text approved by the Inter-Governmental Conference (European Union 2004).

The first concern for the present purpose is that changes made now should not involve the taking of powers, or the establishment of enforceable principles, or the adoption of constitutional rules or procedures, that would preclude, or render unnecessarily difficult, the extension of the Union to the wider world. Further concerns are that there should be movement, however tentative, toward a genuine capacity for common security and foreign policy and hence also for raising the necessary finance, and – what will be argued in the next chapter as very probably necessary for these developments to occur – that there should also be movement in the Union toward more conventional institutions of democratic government.

We should welcome rules and formulas likely to be robust to continuing enlargement of the Union. And, because the compromise reached now can certainly not reflect in full the elements of deepening over foreign and defence policy and tax-raising powers that the argument of this book implies are ultimately essential, we should also welcome built-in flexibility.

Ideally, it would be good to drop the word 'European' from the proposed Article I-1.2, which states that the Union 'shall be open to all European States which respect its values and are committed to promoting them together'. Yet at least this does not explicitly block entry by non-European states. In the lawyers' maxim, the expression of one is not the exclusion of the other.

Elements in the proposals to be welcomed

The element of built-in flexibility

Federal constitutions commonly provide procedures for their own amendment, but there is an underlying presumption that the division of powers between the component states and the centre satisfies current aspirations at the time the particular constitution is framed and is likely to be fairly stable for long periods. By contrast, as with past provisions for the Union and its predecessors, the draft EU Constitution supposes a gap between aspirations – widely held or even formally endorsed – and actual powers. Especially since the Maastricht Treaty, the aspirations to common action have been very broad. Yet, instead of simply giving the Union institutions overriding power in the areas of the two new 'pillars' introduced by Maastricht – Foreign and Security Policy, and Justice and Home Affairs – the draft elaborates rules that would, with sufficient consent among the member-states, allow gradual movement in these directions. Though there may be ambiguities in the documents, this appears to be the case with the two directions of movement considered in this book as crucial: towards a central defence and related foreign policy, and towards adequate autonomy of the central institutions over finance. These are detailed below.

There are a number of differing provisions laid down that can be regarded in the broadest sense as ways of amending the constitution. At one extreme (Article IV-7(2-4)), there is a procedure for calling another convention that can make recommendations for changes to the Treaty that could then be agreed by an intergovernmental conference and sufficiently ratified. There is no limit, it seems, to the kind of change that could be made by this method. Where the European Council deems the amendments proposed not weighty enough, it may decide to skip the convention and move straight to the intergovernmental conference. With more limited scope, Article I-17 gives a general power to the Council – provided that body acts (a) unanimously, (b) on a proposal from the Commission, and (c) with the consent of the Parliament – to take appropriate action 'if action by the Union should prove necessary within the framework of the policies defined in Part III [of the Constitution] to attain one of the objectives set by the Constitution, and the Constitution has not provided the necessary powers'. (Such action is excluded where it would involve harmonization of laws and regulations in areas in which the Constitution precludes harmonization.) This Article in itself, similar to some others in specific areas, provides the possibility of a limited element of deepening: in effect, the governments, if they agree unanimously to do so and are backed by the Commission and Parliament, are able to use the machinery of the Union to take action that might not otherwise be authorized, but only within the scope of objectives and policies laid down in the draft Constitution. More restrictively again in scope, Article IV-7a entails a provision for change (by either allowing the Council to act on qualified majority where previously unanimity had been required or relaxing the terms on which legislation can be passed) if (a) the European Council so decides unanimously, and (b) the Parliament agrees by simple majority of members, (c) no national parliament objects within six months, and (d) in the case of change in the Council voting requirement, there are no military/defence implications. Then, as mentioned below, in the specific matter of foreign and security policy when there are no military/defence implications, there may be a move from unanimous to qualified-majority voting in the Council, on the unanimous decision of the European Council alone (Articles III-20(3), I-39(8)).

The general procedures that the Constitution provides for its own amendment in Article IV-7(2–4) are quite demanding by the standards of federal constitutions, though without any plebiscite requirement. In effect, they depend on the absence of opposition from either government or parliament in any member-state. But certain kinds of change – perhaps most significantly the movement in foreign and security policy from unanimous to qualified-majority voting requirements in the Council – are easier to effect, with the European Council alone being enabled to make the change by unanimous decision.

The explicit right of secession

This (Article I-59) will remove one possible barrier to joining, and possibly provide a safety-valve in conflicts that may arise.

Modest enhancement of the powers of the Parliament in the direction of 'responsible government'

The more powers the Parliament has in relation to the other main constitutional bodies, the more it is likely to be taken seriously by the public and to act responsibly, and also the more readily can Union autonomy over defence/foreign policy and finance become workable. There is probably a slight enhancement of parliamentary power in the arrangement proposed (Articles I-25, I-26) for nomination and approval of the President and Members of the Commission. The President would be nominated by the European Council on a qualified majority, and the Parliament would be able to accept or reject the European Council's candidate. If the decision were to reject, the European Council would be obliged to offer another candidate. The Minister for Foreign Affairs would be nominated by the European Council, but with the agreement of the President-elect of the Commission. To fill the rest of the Commission, the Council 'by common accord with the President-elect' would choose the other members of the Commission, but so that (with the President and Foreign Minister included) there would (in the Commission of 2009–14) be one Commissioner from each member-state. After 2014, there would be two-thirds as many Commissioners as member-states, all member-states represented as nearly as possible equally often over the long term. When the members of the Commission had been nominated, the Parliament could as hitherto approve or reject the Commission as a body, and also subsequently, by a vote of censure, dismiss the whole Commission.

Tentative moves toward the apparatus of a real security and foreign policy

The proposal (Article I-27) to have a Union Foreign Minister, who would be a Vice-President of the Commission, would combine in effect the two posts (High Authority and External Relations Commissioner) that have existed hitherto. The Minister would have a brief (though not an exclusive one) to make proposals on foreign policy and defence (Articles 1-27, I-39, I-40) and to 'conduct' Union common policies on these matters. The proposals would mostly be determined by the European Council or the Council (of Ministers) acting *nem. con.* (though described as 'unanimity', what is required is not quite that), an arrangement that gives only limited scope for common action on such important issues as those on which typically the member governments in recent years have disagreed (Article III-201(1)). However, there would be certain matters (Article III-201(2)) on which the Council of Ministers might act by qualified majority, and on other matters, so long as they did not have 'military or defence implications' (Article III-201(4)), the Minister might, by virtue of a prior unanimous resolution of the European Council, make proposals which could then be determined by a qualified majority vote in the Council (Article I-39(8), III-201(3)). This last provision – similar to the more general one in Article I-17 or Article IV-7a, as recounted above, but not quite so restrictive as either – seems to be a way of allowing by prior consensus some movement away from a hundred-per-cent consensus rule. The member-states might in effect all agree that on some issue or range of issues it was more important for the Union to have the capacity to act than for a minority to retain the power to block action.[1] Perhaps this change does not get us far in itself and is unlikely to work with any highly controversial question unless there is considerable agreement in advance among the governments. But it does open a chink, which may in practice be enlarged as the need for a real foreign policy becomes more evident.

Tentative move toward autonomy in tax-raising powers

Article I-53 appears to be saying that the Council, acting unanimously and with the consent of the Parliament and of all the member-states 'in accordance with their respective constitutional requirements', may both establish new categories of revenue and also set up systems for collecting them. Seriously enhanced Union autonomy in tax-raising powers is probably out of the question politically at the time of writing.

But Article IV-7 on revising the Constitution apparently allows, here as elsewhere, for later movement as outlooks and circumstances change.

Robust definition of a qualified majority in the Council

The Convention's original proposal in Article I-24 was that a decision by 'qualified majority' in the European Council or the Council of Ministers should mean that at least 50 per cent of states, and also states covering 60 per cent of the Union's population, had agreed. These figures were changed by the Inter-Governmental Conference to 55 per cent and 65 per cent, with the 55 per cent becoming 72 per cent unless the motion being considered had been proposed by the Commission or the Foreign Minister (Article I-24). This, despite a few further complications in the arithmetic, is straightforward and rational, immensely more sensible than the bizarre compromises over the votes allocated for qualified-majority purposes hitherto. It would completely obviate the need for the rules on voting to be renegotiated with each enlargement. (It proved, however, more or less by accident, probably the most important stumbling-block to agreement of member governments in late 2003.)

Implied recognition of the fact that not all members may accept the common currency

In Article III-91 and the Protocol on the Euro Group, it is accepted that there must be machinery for the countries that have adopted the euro to make decisions on monetary matters independently of member-states that have not adopted it. No distinction for this purpose is made between countries that are not yet deemed eligible to adopt the euro and those that have decided against it, though the wording of some related Articles could be taken to imply that all those deemed eligible to adopt the euro should do so. For reasons given earlier, we should welcome any fair working arrangement that accepts the fact that some members will adopt the euro and some will not.

General rules for dealing with a measure of 'variable geometry'

As already mentioned, the chapter on 'Enhanced Co-operation' provides for use of the Union's structures to serve agreements on common action in certain areas when those agreements are made by a third or more of member-states.

A survival that is inefficient but undergoing attenuation

Continuation of the national basis for choosing Commissioners

So long as there is any relic of the rule that each member-state must have at least one national as a member of the Commission, each enlargement will cause further embarrassment. But the current proposal (Article I-25), outlined above, seems at least an improvement in terms of efficiency on the one proposed by the Convention and probably quite a reasonable compromise. However, there will still tend to be too many Commissioners as the Union expands further; and the national basis will constrain the choice of talent. Converting the Commission into a more conventional political Cabinet or Executive, responsible to the Parliament, seems the obvious democratic, and potentially efficient, solution. It is stated explicitly that the Commission 'as a body' shall be responsible to the European Parliament (Article I-25.(8)), though that statement in itself may not have much content. The previous position, however, is also re-stated to the effect that, as mentioned above, if the Parliament passes a censure motion on the Commission, the whole Commission must resign. There is thus already some of what we would expect of the relationship between a 'responsible government' and its parliament under a Westminster system. This is not a satisfactory resting-place, but movement is in the right direction.

Riddle or snare

The bill of rights

Part II of the draft Constitution, the Charter of Fundamental Rights of the Union, seems on the face of it ill-advised, and not only from the special standpoint of this book. The impression gained is that an extensive list of 'fundamental rights' has been laid down, but that then the framers have panicked and said that these rights are meant to apply in only very limited circumstances. Thus a number of the clauses asserting rights (for example, Articles II-27, II-28, and II-30) could be taken to imply *only that existing national and Union laws on the subjects mentioned should be implemented*. Then, Articles II-51 and II-52 on interpretation of the Charter seem concerned to limit its application even further. Article II-51(1) says that the provisions of the Charter are addressed 'to Member States only when they are implementing Union law'. And

Article II-52(5) says that the provisions 'which contain principles' should be judicially cognizable only in the interpretation of 'legislative and executive acts taken by Institutions and bodies of the Union, and ... acts of Member States when they are implementing Union law'.

In fact it seems that a large part of the purpose of introducing the Charter was to make clear that the provisions of the European Convention on Human Rights and Fundamental Freedoms are to apply to the EU as an institution (as they apply to its member-state governments) and to the operation of EU law.[2] That perhaps explains some of the paradox. The concern of the framers may have been to make clear that no new fundamental rights were being asserted. Yet in that case dressing the document up as a bill of fundamental rights was misleading and probably a tactical mistake.

The Union's members are all members of the Council of Europe and subject to the European Convention (Council of Europe 2004), which has been adopted by some countries into their domestic law and has longstanding and workable judicial implementation machinery. It might have been more sensible to refer to the European Convention for the rights asserted, or even to attach it to the Constitution. (This Charter does in fact refer to the European Convention for definitions of some of the rights that it proclaims.)

Including the Charter in the draft Constitution probably achieves the worst of all worlds. Arguably it adds little or nothing to enforceable rights, apart perhaps from those of Union employees, not hitherto a particularly oppressed class, but at the same time it risks a hornets' nest of legal uncertainties, and gives the impression, to those who are worried about extra costly regulation and lawsuits, that the draft Constitution would be introducing a big new crop of material for bureaucrats and lawyers.

However, not all the rights asserted in the draft Charter are also listed in the European Convention. From the particular viewpoint of this book, it is also undesirable that, under cover of universal rights, demands come to be introduced that can only in relatively rich countries be seriously contemplated as general, enforceable rules. Yet parental leave and paid maternity leave, on birth or adoption, and generally the full gamut of welfare-state provisions, are prescribed in Articles II-33 and II-34. Also, in a bizarre extension of the notion of fundamental rights, 'Everyone has the right of access to a free placement service', says Article II-29. Where the economic and institutional conditions exist to make this style of state welfare benefits possible, they will probably happen in any case, and the precise form of welfare-state provision needs surely to be left to national choice. No Charter will make universal cash benefits happen where they are effectively impossible.

Inclusion of measures that only rich countries can hope to implement – as among the fundamentals – need be of no concern in itself to those who want to keep the Union as a club for the relatively rich. But, if we want to widen its scope, we need to drop the apparent demand that everyone should have West-European-style social security. It is not good enough to add that we didn't really mean it. If extreme poverty in poor countries is to be remedied, this will come about by a combination of general rises in income, supplemented by external aid of various sorts, and internal institutions that provide appropriate incentives, property-rights, and safety-nets consistent with existing average-income levels. It will not be remedied by ambiguous grounds for court cases against unnamed respondents. On all scores it would be better to drop the Charter, which, in spite of the fact that it would probably have very little effect on conditions of life, might cause the Treaty to fail its ratification and referendum tests, or, if it were passed, be used to block or delay Union expansion. If it is necessary to state ideals, why not be content with appending the European Convention for the Protection of Human Rights and Fundamental Freedoms, a serious document with a record of implementation, and one to which states in the Union, including the 2004 entrants, are all officially committed in any case? In short, there is already a quite reliable and discriminating watchdog. This new one under consideration has a bark fit to clear the neighbourhood, but the suppliers mutter that its teeth have been removed.

It is hard to escape the conclusion that the Charter of Fundamental Rights in its present form would be better deleted. Whatever needs to be done so that the European Convention would apply to the Union as an institution can be expressed presumably in a few lines embodied in an unpretentious clause.

The principal remaining deficiencies

Institutions for foreign and defence policy

From the standpoint of this book, that is the key competence that the Union needs. Yet it is clear that the governments and peoples would on no account have approved right now the machinery necessary for a genuine Union foreign and defence policy. This would require an executive (a) carrying the authority that would spring either from direct popular election or from possessing the confidence of a majority in the elected chamber of the Parliament, (b) empowered to act at its discretion diplomatically so long as it remained in place, and (c) able to command the Union's armed forces as it might see the need. These ingredients, even if only for foreign policy and defence purposes, would have no hope of general acceptance in 2003–5. The Union Foreign Minister, who might sometimes be able to generate a consensus among twenty-five governments, and in some cases might be allowed to work on the strength of a qualified majority of them, was probably as far as the Constitution framers could go. But there is no reason to think that further movement in the institutions is precluded if the present draft Constitution is accepted. A later convention under Article IV-7 could always move things along if enough of the stakeholders were willing. Neither the Treaty at present on the table nor its absence would freeze a particular set of arrangements.

Lack of autonomous financial power

In the proposals the Union still appears, as outlined above, to depend on what *sources* of finance governments will unanimously allow it to have. On the budget, however, and by implication spending, arrangements would be not quite so restrictive. The budget (Article III-310) would be approved by consensus between the Council of Ministers and the Parliament. In case of dispute, the Council would decide by qualified majority, the Parliament also by more than a simple majority of votes cast. If conciliation between the two failed, and each stuck to its position by the required majority, the Council would be asked to prepare another budget. Failing final agreement, the month-by-month makeshift based mainly on the previous year's authorization would prevail (Article III-311). As with the appointment of the President of the Commission, Council and Parliament would both be involved, but the Council, which alone would be entitled to make a completely new proposal in case of deadlock, would probably have the stronger hand. On spending, this implies, a qualified majority of the governments would have in the last resort to agree to anything new. For the eventual role we are envisaging for the Union, the Union institutions will probably need to be less inhibited by state governments in relating finance raised and spent to union concerns. But again the arrangements mooted in the draft Constitution would be open to later development.

★★★

In conclusion, much of the movement proposed in these elements of the document is in the right direction from the viewpoint of this book, even if it is often extremely tentative. The bill of rights should ideally be replaced by a clause making clear the application to the Union and its laws of the European Convention. No doubt change will continue.

Notes

1. It is not immediately clear whether one unanimous resolution by the European Council could authorize action in the field concerned by qualified-majority vote in the Council *for the indefinite future*. The commentary on the draft Constitution produced by the European Parliament delegation to the Convention (European Parliament 2004) says that the broadly similar general provision for extending qualified-majority voting in some area of Union competence (presumably Article IV-7a) does indeed apply 'for the future'.

2. This was the gist of the explanation of the main function of the Charter of Fundamental Rights kindly provided to the writer, in answer to a question at a public meeting, by Neil MacCormick, Regius Professor of Public Law in Edinburgh, who, as a Member of the European Parliament, had taken part in the Convention.

Chapter 7

Routes from here to there

Urgently needed: a (real) common foreign and security policy for the European Union

So far the discussion in this book of the role of the EU has concentrated on its possible long-term calling as a foundation for a limited global confederation. Yet the events of early 2003 have made the case for a common defence and foreign policy on the part of the Union important not only on that ground but also as a matter of more immediate geopolitics. A vital step on the long path to effective world organization would have an immediate value of its own.

Security policy, with the related elements of foreign policy – the most vital area for unification and the deepening of co-operation in governmental mode – is also the most controversial. Defence is naturally held to be an essential, perhaps *the* essential, function of the state. Patriotism, national mythology, and self-image tend to be bound up with military effort and achievement.

Yet at the same time the avoidance of war (without sacrifice of the safeguards and security that alone can, on a rational and responsible assessment, make the possibility and threat of war seem worthwhile) is the most fundamental reason for seeking a global political organization. It is the central objective of responsible statecraft.

In the European Union as it now is, development of the other activities that we have identified as essential areas of eventual governmental integration for the world are likely to meet no great obstacles. A justiciable regime on human rights is already in existence through the institutions of the Council of Europe, and it has generally been taken seriously in EU countries. Effective co-operation on cross-border environmental issues has given rise to considerable common legislation, with more to be expected. 'Environmental protection has been identified through opinion polls', writes Bainbridge (2002: 163) 'as an area in which there is a consistently high level of public support for action at Union level.' There is also reason to think that arrangements for funding Union activities, including assistance to relatively disadvantaged areas, will develop as the needs of the activities authorized at Union level expand.

But so far a common foreign and security policy is little more than a paper aspiration. There may be plenty of consultation, but that is a long way from a policy. On several of the crucial foreign and defence questions since 1990 – Croatia, Bosnia, Kosovo, and most strikingly Iraq – the large EU members took more or less divergent positions. That this should quite often be so seems in retrospect almost unavoidable while the individual states have the ultimate power and right of decision. Their governments will see things differently from one another. Sometimes purely national interests, or supposed interests, or sentiments such as those attaching to historic alliances, will enter in. Foreign and defence questions are after all potentially the most important. Why should any government allow its own judgement in these matters to be simply overridden? And who in any case would have a claim to override it? So far in the EU there is no larger authority that has been authorized to speak and act for the whole in this domain.

This is a journey in which there is no real halfway house. Either there is a common foreign and security policy, with a single constituted authority empowered to decide its content and limits, or there is not. In the only context we can contemplate, it must be a democratically constituted authority: presumably either directly elected by the people of the Union at large or else responsible to an assembly elected by them. But it must be an entity that does not depend for its authority to act on the universal consent, or even perhaps the majority consent, of state governments. It must be a creature of an identifiable majority of the people of the Union, subject sooner or later to recall by them or by their representatives if it displeases too many of them, but not an agency that is obliged to remain inactive if it should fail to achieve a consensus or near-consensus among twenty-five or thirty-five or fifty governments. It is precisely because governments differ, not because they agree, that we need a common authority, one that is not dependent upon their individual assent.

The importance of a common defence and foreign policy right now

I believe that the strongest of cases can be made within the European Union now – independently of any aspiration to move toward world confederation – for constituting this community of 400 million or so people in such a way that, at any time, it can speak with one voice on foreign and security questions: so that there is an official European position, however controversial it may be among the Union's people, one that will be backed with European funding and in the last resort with European force.

It is difficult to discuss this question today without reference to the USA. Because of the military supremacy of America, the significance of European states, jointly or severally, revolves in large part around how they respond to American policy: in supporting it, modifying it, opposing it, or even possibly leading it. At the time of writing, the division of official Europe over American policy toward Iraq has been striking. Yet the members and aspirant members of the EU have had a number of objectives and relevant values in common with the US. All – probably all governments, and, with few exceptions, people – wanted Saddam to give up weapons of mass destruction if he had them, and all would have been happy if he had stood aside and were glad at his going. All the states, on a more general plane – despite some aberrations of their own – recognize a common interest in a stable and prosperous world, in democracy, human rights, and good government. Admittedly, in trade policy, the US and the countries of Europe sometimes seem to be quarrelling in negative-sum fashion like dogs over bones. Yet in matters of high security – however much each may have infuriated the other, however much locally emotive issues may have distorted the policy of particular states – we can broadly say that, until the start of the new century, the governments of the US and those of the nine pre-1981members of the EU had for some decades differed at most over means toward the same broad objectives.

Since 2001, this is no longer clearly the case. Two of the three main foreign policy impulses acting on the Bush administration have run counter to values and objectives apparently prevailing among the political classes in Western Europe, even in those countries whose governments supported the US in the Iraq war. These two correspond to what Bobbitt (2002: 246–53, 265–9) calls 'the New Nationalism' and 'the New Evangelism'. The former is the one evident in the Bush foreign policy as presented before the 2000 election, with a tendency to restrict international engagements to those that had an immediate and manifest direct bearing on the survival and prosperity of the US itself: elements of isolationism insofar as that is possible in the present century. The latter is the doctrine propounded by the 'neoconservatives': with its calling to establish democracy everywhere, by force if necessary, regardless of circumstances and politics on the ground. Both can dispose their followers to ignore consensual international law in matters of war and peace; to downgrade international institutions generally, rejecting any constraints they may impose; and to disregard the values and sensibilities of other nations, either setting no value on allies or expecting them to do as they are told. Neither of these two policy models will necessarily become established as dominant in the US; there is of course a third impulse, more in accord with past US policy since 1945, favouring more reciprocal relations with allies and more respect for international law and institutions. At the time of the Suez War in 1956, it was America that stood for international legalities and proprieties against their disregard by France and Britain. But at the time of writing the embedding of a stance that attracts the antipathy of prevailing sentiment in Europe – one destructive of any consensual international order – cannot be ruled out. If that happens, Europe's public and its governments in general will in this respect recognize interests in conflict with critically important elements of US policy. There will be fundamental differences as well as fundamental agreements.

So Europe may be much more ambivalent over US leadership than before. On particular issues the continent and the Union may well be deeply divided as in early 2003. When an alternative to US policy needs to be taken seriously, it may well be difficult for a divided Europe or its components to have an effective dialogue with the US and so to achieve a compromise or a resolution of differences.

Is a single official Union foreign-and-security voice, or a Babel of official foreign-and-security voices, likely to exercise the more salutary influence in this new situation? The Babel will almost inevitably have less influence, but is there a presumption that this lesser influence will be somehow on balance be better in its direction, and moreover so much better as to make up for its weaker force? It is hard to see that this is likely to be so. Unless we believe that official France or official Britain, say, is generally and consistently much more right than the rest – so that, even as a solitary voice within a discordant chorus, it will often make an irreplaceable contribution – the contention is not convincing. The interest of France or the interest of Britain, like the interest of each other member-state, will be represented, under the arrangement we are envisaging, in a Union parliament and also in much that they may still be able to do on their own. For many purposes other than security policy and the directly related elements of foreign policy, France and Britain will continue to conduct their own affairs. The question is simply whether in security and foreign affairs the counsel, linked to the bargaining-power, of a French or British government, or of one of the others, is so valuable that it cannot be adequately replaced by the influence of French or British opinion and wisdom within the security-and-foreign machinery of the Union.

It is surely a plausible view, for those not systematically hostile to the US but uneasy about its heavy dominance, that the world would gain from the presence of a further comparably large and potentially powerful entity sharing many of America's broad values and objectives but sometimes making different political judgements. In the US we are, after all, dealing not with a monolith but with a heavily disputed policy arena. Those in the world who think that the US is generally, though not invariably, right will be glad to have a single, weighty European security entity that can offer its critical support. Those who think that the US is generally wrong will be reassured at the presence of a substantial actor, powerful enough to be taken seriously, that will exercise sympathetic restraint. Those who expect from the US a mixture of good and bad judgements should welcome the advent of another large power in the democratic camp whose second opinion cannot be ignored.

At the moment it seems that Germany, Italy, and the Low Countries – probably some of the forthcoming East European members, possibly also Spain and Portugal – could move fairly readily into those institutions that would make a genuinely common foreign and security policy possible. France (despite the rhetoric) would be equivocal. Britain, the Nordics, probably Poland and Greece, possibly Ireland, would be less enthusiastic. If that is more or less the division, it cuts right across the 2003 faultline over Iraq.

On the most optimistic view, the genuinely governmental constitutional prerequisite for a common foreign and security policy cannot be expected for some years. The sceptics are influential enough for the time being to prevent a confederal solution from being adopted in the form of a real workable mechanism. The most that can be hoped in the dealings over the draft Constitution of 2004 is that the issue should be left potentially open, so that the Union is allowed and able to respond to changing opinion and events on this most important of constitutional questions. The tentative arrangement proposed in the draft Constitution, for a Union Foreign Minister, who could have certain classes of her or his proposals determined by qualified majority in the Council and in the extreme might be asked (by unanimous Council vote) to make proposals in other categories that could be decided by qualified majority, seems a small move in the right direction.

On a slightly longer perspective, the European movement might be persuaded to accept that 'a more perfect union' – a union that caters best to the needs of those within and without – does not primarily require a common postal service or tax system or currency, or common rules on working time or on minimum wages or immigration or safety in toys. Some of these are possibly desirable, some definitely not, some dubious or indifferent. What the Union requires first, and as soon as possible, is pooled defence and the capacity for taking a corporate position on foreign policy.

This of course does not imply universal agreement within the Union, just as having a single British foreign policy does not imply that everyone in Britain agrees with it. But it does suppose a real political executive – at least over this area of government – probably responsible to, at least depending for legislation and finance on, a European Parliament, the two jointly exercising, at least in this one field, powers approximating those normally held by the executive and legislature of a European democracy: a real democratic government, if only for defence and related aspects of foreign policy.

For the Union, in the first decades of this century, to play a salutary role in world affairs commensurate with its human resources and income, it must be able to take an effective position in this one overwhelmingly important area. Conveniently, the same condition holds for its capacity to form the seed-crystal of an eventual new world order. And in turn the precondition for this ability to form and pursue a common policy is that it should, at least for the exercise of this one set of powers, have the political institutions of a democratic state.

Retained national identities in the foreign arena

Numerous questions would arise over how far, in this new position, individual member-states' identities would remain recognized and active in the international arena. In all matters related to military commitments and alliances, the Union would have to speak with one voice. There could be only one veto power for it in the Security Council, and presumably no more than one Security Council place. But any member-state could well keep its own identifiable military units within the Union forces and have a recognized interest in them; and it might have the discretion to use them, say in humanitarian interventions and peacekeeping, subject to Union approval. Furthermore, in the UN General Assembly, where much of the resolution is aspirational rather than legislative or executive in nature, and in the Specialized Agencies, where most of the business is independent of military questions, the individual states could continue to be represented, possibly financing the Specialized Agencies individually. (The changes proposed could be partly counterproductive in the near future if they diminished the UN as a forum, or deprived the Specialized Agencies of the individual contributions of major nations.) States could also keep their places in the governing institutions of the World Bank, and some of them also in those of the IMF at least so long as the single currency and single monetary control were not imposed as a genuine essential of Union membership. (In fact, anomalous as it may seem, the euro countries do now retain their individual Governor positions and their individual or shared Executive Director positions in the IMF.)

Each member-state would naturally keep a foreign office for those matters of international dealing that did not directly bear on war and peace or on other matters under sole Union control: potentially for trade promotion, cultural relations, financial and technical assistance aside from that offered by the Union, and conventions of various sorts on subjects outside the Union's exclusive control.

NATO

The question of NATO membership is highly emotive among some British eurosceptics. Not only, they seem to say, must membership be retained but it is also *lèse-majesté* at best to attempt to form any of the European members into a single, more integrated force. NATO appears to be deemed in these circles unthinkable other than as an alliance of a dominant power and satellites. Yet there is no obvious reason why a militarily united European entity should not replace a group of existing members, keeping a part in the common NATO command structure if that seems appropriate. It is not clear why European countries should be less eligible members of the alliance if they combine.

A borders and cultural-autonomy convention and tribunal

It has been argued above in Chapter 5 both that an ultimate world polity (or any governmental union designed to form its core) would need to have binding obligations upon member-states for resort to institutions designed to help settle the disputes over borders and cultural allegiances that are responsible for so much tension, armaments, and actual warfare, and also that the world needs 'quasi-voluntary' consensual arrangements for the same purpose now. The character and rationale of the proposal, essentially the same whether under the auspices of the UN or of the EU or its successor, are examined further here.

The UN agreement could be of such a form that individual states would have the opportunity to ratify their adherence to it, ratification implying that they would follow the procedures laid down in the convention. Once a certain number of members had ratified the convention, the tribunal could be brought into existence. Those states agreeing to subject themselves to the convention would naturally encourage others to do likewise.

The convention would bind the signatory states to submit disputes over borders, and claims for self-determination or for cultural autonomy on the part of particular groups of people, to a tribunal that would have powers of investigation, conciliation, and arbitration: it would bind them at least to enter into a process of exploration and discussion under the auspices of an independent institution. There might be two levels of adherence to the UN convention, with an advanced form under which signatories would bind themselves (possibly with certain qualifications) actually to adopt any arbitral decisions of the tribunal. A claim of dispute could be brought by a government or by a sufficiently large body of individuals.

A major part of the hope attached to the propounding of the convention and the adherence of significant powers to it would be that it would encourage a cultural change: an advance of the idea that boundary disputes were not a test of virility for any state or people but rather an unavoidable accident that had to be met in some compromise between the fairest and the most generally acceptable way possible; that borders drawn at some time in the past on maps did not have a sacred character; and that 'possessing' more people or territory did not make a state or nation any better. If large, powerful states with prestige were seen to accept this entirely sensible view, others might recognize the virtue in it and follow.

Regardless of how much or how little progress has been made in the European Union toward a common defence and foreign policy, either it should set up its own convention and tribunal to which members would be bound to adhere, probably committing themselves to adopt any arbitral decisions, or, if a satisfactory UN convention for the same purpose has come into being, it should require its own members to accept the fullest version of the obligations laid down there. Either way, there will be an additional condition implied in EU membership.

A convention and tribunal of this sort will probably be a necessary element in a number of situations for keeping the peace, even under confederal institutions that for defence purposes cover all or a large slice of the world. This is because it will serve as a damper on the emotions that lead to unofficial wars. Without the political integration provided by confederal institutions, it will also be needed as an important contributor to peace in the immediate and foreseeable future.

Yet composing it in workable form can be no easy matter. No general law is likely to be devised that can serve in itself to settle disputes of this kind satisfactorily. A usable convention would need to depend very largely on consultative and conciliatory procedures. In every act of self-determination involving the movement of borders, there is likely to be a local minority at least as intensely opposed to the change as the majority is in favour, and possibly more so.

Two considerations, one evaluative and one pragmatic, potentially in conflict, would need to be observed. One is that existing borders are not sacrosanct and that it is the will and interest of the people in the area affected that should take priority. The other is that changing borders against the will of some of those affected, even if they are a minority, can easily release much more open resentment and trouble than leaving them as they are in despite of the will of the majority. Change for the worse, concrete or symbolic, is always likely to cause more offence than leaving a comparably bad situation as it is. A loss will mean more to the loser than an apparently equal gain to the winner. The-devil-they-know for the majority will probably be less malign than the-devil-they-don't-know for the minority. Those who want a particular boundary to shift so that they come to lie on the other side of it probably feel much less intensely about it on the whole than those who do not want it to change.

So, even if governments and the 'public opinion' of the majority in the various states had abandoned all chauvinism and territory-fixation, big dilemmas would remain. It is no solution to take some level of administrative unit and declare, regardless of circumstances, that the majority in each such area will determine on which side of a state border the unit will lie. Sometimes there may be more-or-less acceptable lines, but they are not necessarily the boundaries of existing administrative units. If there is to be any change in the border between state A and state B, it will have to come as a result of something fairly close to a consensus in the area affected.

If no coherent line can initially be drawn that has a reasonable chance of leaving those on both sides of it tolerably satisfied, then everything else available should be thrown onto the table to mollify any displeased minority: autonomy for their area, their own schools, official use of their own language, right to fly their preferred flag, explicit application in the local courts of provisions of relevant international conventions.

If it is still the case that no neat line can be drawn, then ragged lines and enclaves may be considered, provided the two states affected are prepared to act with sense and allow free trade and free movement of people into and out of any enclave. The recent tendency toward inter-state treaties featuring free trade and sometimes free labour movement within the area covered makes such solutions increasingly feasible and decreasingly inefficient. A principle of cultural autonomy would assert, for example, the claims of those minorities left on the wrong side of any line to have some control over such matters as their own schools.

The main operational point of the convention would be to refer to an internationally run process any grievance or dispute that might possibly involve borders and the extent of jurisdictions. Where the border questions concerned were purely legal–historical rather than resulting from popular feeling, they could be subject to a legal decision (with possible reference to the International Court of Justice) or to arbitration. Where they derived principally from people's preferences, the process for settling them would be primarily consultation and conciliation. The value of visibly impartial mediators and monitors, from right outside the arena, has been seen in the Northern Ireland peace process, and perhaps, however imperfectly and inconclusively, in Palestine–Israel and Sri Lanka.

There might in any particular case be no satisfactory answer. But if the effect of the convention was that say on average one case in two of those that would otherwise have led, or had already led, to fighting or terrorism was instead brought at least to a tolerable conclusion for all parties, that would be a valuable achievement.

Why would any state agree to be subject to these processes? Because wars and rebellions are painful, embarrassing, and costly. And because 'losing' territory or people through an impartial and rational process, voluntarily accepted, to which many of the great powers have themselves submitted, need no longer be humiliating. Increasingly often perhaps, as with the Irish and British governments over Northern Ireland during the past few years, the sovereign authorities will be concerned – virtually to the exclusion of all else – to reach a settlement widely acceptable among majority and minority communities. Losing or gaining land and people in the old-fashioned imperialist sense will not be a consideration for the sovereign powers.

Among pre-2004 EU members, and those entering in 2004, it may seem now that there is little prospect that a convention of the sort will be necessary – or at least that it will be necessary for the purpose of preventing actual interstate warfare. But, with the next few likely or possible batches of entrants, headed by the rest of the Balkans, trouble among members over borders and cultural rights is more than a conceptual possibility. The Union will not tolerate cultural or national repression within its domain, and it is essential that aspirant members recognize and accept the implications of this before they enter. Some of these problems will have no entirely satisfactory solutions. What can be hoped for, or aspired to, is the best possible trade-off among the claims of people with diverse loyalties.

Next steps

Given that a common foreign and security policy will not come about immediately, what are the most promising first steps from where we are in 2005? The priority is probably to move toward an Executive that can be regarded, according to the canons prevailing in Europe today, as having full democratic legitimacy. The Executive initially may have very limited powers in the foreign-and-security area. Indeed, those powers are unlikely to be ceded in any significant degree unless there is first an authority of recognizably democratic provenance to exercise them.

The Commission as constituted at the time of writing in 2004, with its members nominated individually by governments, does not meet this test. (It would come closer, though still not close enough, under the draft Constitution.) Though constituted as a form of executive, it is not in the usual sense democratically responsible. The European Parliament does not choose the Commission or its individual members, though it is supposed to be consulted about the choice of Commission

President, and under the draft Constitution it would share selection of the President with the European Council, albeit as a junior partner. It can, however, dismiss the Commission *en bloc* or refuse to endorse it upon its nomination. The Council, the other ostensible candidate for executive status, is an assembly of government representatives all of whom have other pressing responsibilities. At the time of writing it has no formal leadership other than the automatically rotating six-month chairmanship, though, for the European Council (the meeting of heads of government), this would be altered under the draft Constitution. It is hampered by the need for a fairly high degree of consensus, while at the same time its members' allegiances and standpoints are primarily those of the states to which they belong. It could not readily develop into a working political executive that had both to define policies and, through its individual members, to take day-to-day decisions.

The draft Constitution of 2004 (see Appendix to Chapter 6) proposes some steps that tend to make the Commission more 'democratic' (at least more parliamentary) in its method of selection. It would also allow the members of the Council to choose a leader in the form of a non-rotating Council President, who would presumably have that post as his or her only responsibility and would not be representing any particular member-state's government. It would create the post of Union Foreign Minister, a member of the Commission as well as an executive servant of the Council, and having powers of initiation: another move out of which, on the face of it, a workable ministerial system of determining foreign and defence policy might gradually be developed. It would allow the Parliament to veto the Council's candidate for President of the Commission before the other members were nominated, and then permit the President some constrained choice over the other members of the Commission, including the Union Foreign Minister. Under these proposals we would have further rudiments of a machine that might subsequently be activated in one of several ways including the one broadly outlined in Chapter 6. These steps should emphatically be welcomed.

Widening: favourable conditions and critical paths

The hope behind the project explored in this book must be that the readiness to widen on the part of a Union that is also in the process of becoming 'governmental' in certain crucial respects will attract outsiders, encouraging, where necessary, the forces within them that tend toward observance of the standards of democracy, rule-of-law, human rights, and respect for minorities, that the Union demands of entrants.

Joining, it may be hoped, will become, or continue to be, a mark of distinction – the fashion – while at the same time bringing visible and concrete advantages: not only the bonus of rich and open markets but also the capacity to pursue perceived 'historical injustices', and to be defended, without the burden of huge and costly armaments and with a reduced risk of war.

So long as military power is needed – that is to say, as long as the confederation is not universal – the sheer size of the Union will enable it to deliver the protection that arises from being part of a major military power, without imposing big per capita costs for the privilege. The diversity of the Union, in outlook and national mythology, will also mean that it is likely to use its military power sparingly and not to rush into conflicts on emotional grounds.

The poor among potential member-nations will also probably see the advantages of being able to bargain, rather than simply to plead, for financial help over their most pressing social needs and for open access to affluent markets; while the rich will recognize that sharing in such a polity need not demand intolerable, or even perhaps very noticeable, sacrifices. (This happy conjunction is made possible by the huge differences, especially on exchange-rate comparisons, in real incomes and labour costs between rich and poor nations. Trivial sacrifices on the part of the former can be turned into big bonuses for the latter. The safety mechanism proposed in Chapter 6 should serve to prevent the process from going too far to be acceptable.)

Outsiders may also recognize that the desirable elements of national and local autonomy are not impaired by the Union. Local and national traditions may be followed except where they conflict with human-rights conventions. Local distinctiveness need be no more diminished than is likely to happen in any case under the influence of international traffic and communication. Such, we may hope, is the picture that Union membership will come to present to potential members.

At the same time, the hope for those already inside must be that each new accession of members, like each new element of necessary deepening, will reveal itself as tolerable, as has broadly been the case with the European Union and its predecessors so far. The East European and Mediterranean entrants of 2004 will quite probably be so satisfactorily accommodated that there can be sympathetic consideration later in the decade for admittance of some or all of the rest of south-east Europe and Turkey. That prospect in turn may prompt further constitutional changes (for example, over the number of Commissioners and the mode of choosing them) that are more appropriate for achieving democratic responsibility and efficiency in an ever-expanding association. (The provisions of the 2004 draft Constitution on the number, roles, and mode of selection, of Commissioners, as outlined in the Appendix to Chapter 6, could hardly be considered a permanent solution.)

We have seen this process continuing so far: new states wanting to join and gradually coming to be regarded as eligible. Twenty years earlier there would have been overwhelming reasons – on one side or both – why not only most of the ten entrants of 2004 but also the three entrants of 1995 could not have joined. As recently as 1998, Slovakia and the three Baltics were not in the front row of aspirants. Eligibility can apparently emerge quite rapidly.

Rumania, Bulgaria, and Turkey are already in a sense in the queue and in fact took part in the Future of Europe Convention. Albania and the remaining successor states to Yugoslavia must inevitably be considered possibles. Few of these eight to eleven states (is Bosnia one or two; are Serbia, Montenegro, and Kosovo one, two, or three?) could be admitted tomorrow. There is still unfinished business in what used to be Yugoslavia. Turkey has to complete the reforms begun so hopefully: in abolishing torture (convincingly), fully validating the legalization of peaceful Kurdish political activity, probably giving autonomy to the main Kurdish areas, certainly giving full cultural rights to Kurds everywhere. But much of this is under way or seems imminent.

And the necessary changes may come quickly. The death of Tudjman, the fall of Milosevic, the *de facto* separation of Kosovo, the reforms mooted from late 2002 (and gradually being implemented) by the AK government in Turkey: all these have altered the omens. It is probably not utopian to expect most, if not all, of these south-eastern states to be in the EU by 2010 or soon after, giving a possible population somewhere in the region of 570 million.

Need it be utopian to imagine the process as going further? If all the obstacles to extending the Union from the Shannon to the Euphrates have been overcome, why should it stop there?

Crossing the River Bug

On the ground that we live in an era in which impossibles, good and bad, suddenly become actual, I venture to suggest where we may look for further widening in the century's second decade, once we have established by experience that the Union, with whatever form and degree of deepening it has by then achieved, can manage with the south-eastern states and Turkey included. The neighbours that could not then be ignored are the Ukraine and Russia – and Belarus once it showed stirrings of democracy and the rule of law. Ukraine would probably wish to join and has already made noises in that direction. Russia might.

Clearly there is quite a lot of change that we would expect before either of these two big states could be a suitable partner, change that goes beyond the formal democracy that exists: a measure of economic stability, clear establishment of the rule of law and media freedom, lessening of mafia influence, and, in the case of Russia, a settled and acceptable way of dealing with moves for secession or greater auton-omy among the Republics and Regions.

These are large agenda, some of them likely to be seen as sacrifices by those in power, but stranger things have happened. It would seem incredible if Russia, the core of a recent superpower, with its huge stock of highly educated manpower and technical know-how, to say nothing of its natural resources, should remain in the state of wide-spread material misery and social impotence to which the first decade of 'transition' consigned it.

Provided the entry conditions were fulfilled, would Russia itself be willing? It is hard to predict of course, but there are at least pos-sible reasons why government and people might see advantages in joining. Given the generally humiliating experience of Russia through the 1990s, it seems likely that self-image will play a large part in deter-mining how the issue is seen. Suppose the Balkans and Turkey were already members and that Ukraine (possibly also Belarus) was either actually inside or else willing, and becoming eligible, to join. No matter how far recovered from the traumas of the 1990s, Russia is unlikely, by 2015 say, to fill the role of a hyperpower. Its attempts at hegem-ony in Central Asia and the Caucasus, when they were not disasters, have been mainly of nuisance value rather than evidence of a power-ful guiding force. Virtually all the rest of Slav and Orthodox Europe would, in this scenario, be already in the Union or on the brink of joining. Russia on entering the Union would be the biggest individual member by far, with about a fifth of the total population. With Russia included, the Union would probably have twice the population of the US and a higher total income. If able to act as an entity in defence and foreign policy, it would be a potential superpower, able, if it chose, to compare with the US in military strength before very long.

Without Russia, the Union (even without Ukraine) would have something like four times the population of Russia and very much more than four times the income. On the score of self-image, the advice 'If you can't beat them, join them' could have some appeal. All this is apart from any trade-and-aid advantages for a poorer country of joining the Union.

In the constitutional arrangements we have supposed in Chapter 6, Russian Federation members of the Union Parliament would dispose of nearly a fifth of the total votes. The Russian government would still have jurisdiction over a large range of matters; would (on the draft Constitution's 55-per-cent/65-per-cent voting rule, or on any other likely to be devised) have a larger weight than any other member in the Council, which we have supposed to continue as at least an upper chamber; and would still operate as a national government in a number of international arenas.

Russia versus common defence: widening or deepening first?

Should Russia be admitted *before* or *after* the Union adopts the institutions for giving it a genuine defence and foreign policy?

Of course, the choice may not present itself in that form. Events may constrain the sequence. But, on the face of it, moving to common defence arrangements first is likely to facilitate both moves: it will be easier without Russia; and attracting Russia will be easier after it has happened. A single voice on defence-related foreign policy must mean one permanent Security Council place and veto. It will be hard enough to persuade France and Britain to cast their veto powers into the common pool without having to do the same for Russia simultaneously. On the other hand, Russia's motive for joining the Union may well be stronger once the Union is a considerable power.[1] From the viewpoint of the main argument put in this book, that is another ground for hastening the climactic move to the institutions that are needed to effect a common defence and foreign policy.

Opening to Africa

A further possible direction of widening in, say, the second decade of the century may seem at first glance bizarre but ought to be considered on its merits. It may very well be that around 2015, or even sooner, some of the southern African states – South Africa, Botswana perhaps, maybe others too by then – can be judged to have the institutions that would enable them to join. Of course they might not choose to do so. There is an African Union, though of no great significance so far. Nevertheless, an ideal of African unity exists, and South Africa is for many reasons the obvious candidate to play a leading role in any form of African association. Membership of a union springing from Europe with aspirations to confederation might well seem inconsistent with a more important task on the home continent. But after all the union based in Europe exists, rich and substantial, maybe much more substantial as well as more cosmopolitan by the time the question arises. Substantive African union has proved so far a rather tenuous hope. Given any form in which it is likely to materialize in the foreseeable future (cultural, technological, consultative), participation in it will probably not be inconsistent with membership of a union in the form envisaged here that has happened to start in Europe but is explicitly loosening its European moorings. A *pan*-African intergovernmental association has, like the UN, to accommodate virtually every state in its region, however disreputably governed, and to adapt to its least amenable member's disposition to co-operate. If a choice must be made, Africans arguably have less need of another mini-UN without resources than of a (rich) union with entry standards that will, if they meet those standards, be prepared to deal with them on equal terms. On the whole African nations need as many links as possible of mutual benefit with the affluent part of the world, links that are demanding as well as generous. Of course they should not settle for whatever offer is available. But it would make sense not to reject any offer, without consideration and without any attempt to negotiate, simply on the ground that it came from an institution begun in Europe.

So long as the gates are kept wide open to any African state that meets certain well-defined standards of political institutions and practice – the same standards as those applied in Europe itself – it can plausibly be argued that the aim is not to select African countries for their usefulness to Europe but rather to create a genuine partnership with Africa. It has been suggested above that, even if and when a genuinely common defence and defence-related foreign policy is established, the individual states should retain many of their international links and roles. The more genuinely cosmopolitan and global the Union becomes, the greater the variety of cultural and regional links individual members will have. It is clear that any African states entering would need to be able to retain their African connections. And it has been stressed that membership in the union being considered would be explicitly soluble; entering it would not be an irrevocable move. Symbolically the way in for any African countries that met the entry tests might be eased if the relationship between the EU and the seventy-eight or so African, Caribbean and Pacific (ACP) states associated with it were to become more genuinely reciprocal.

But why look next to Africa for additional members rather than to some other region such as South-east Asia or South Asia? Probably what is in fact needed at the stage considered is an announcement or sign that the Union is potentially open to any state that meets the entry conditions. But, because they are so numerous, African states are likely to include at least a few that, now or soon, can be considered eligible and may at the same time be willing. And on the whole it is African countries and those of similar type – often small and primary-export-dominated as well as poor – that on economic grounds most *need* integration – an integration of mutual responsibility – with richer nations. Admittedly those likely to be the first admitted will probably be the ones that need it least. But their membership can provide the rest with another source of hope, and a further reason for aspiration to better governance, in situations that must often look extremely unpromising.

Calculus of net gain from joining

What might be hoped is that a succession of states will come – one by one or in groups – to see the gains from joining as exceeding the costs. Then each will join if it meets the criteria. Otherwise it may take action toward meeting them. As the Union grows, it becomes an increasingly firm security safeguard. And at the same time its cost of defence per inhabitant probably falls, especially as potential assailants become members. Any heavily armed state that joins probably acquires thereby more secure protection at a lower price. On rational calculation of the public benefit, it is easy to see why the security offer might be attractive for a small African country. But even a large Asian country, especially one that considered itself under external threat, might well perceive a net gain too.

Consider the choices faced by Pakistan and India even if say thirty years from now they have not resolved their dispute and are still in the same hugely costly and dangerous military confrontation they have maintained for the last fifty-five years. As suggested below, the continuation of the conflict raises political-emotional obstacles to incorporation of the parties in the union, but at the same it greatly increases the concrete advantages to themselves of joining.

Whoever controls matters then in Pakistan (the weaker party and the one that has always considered itself aggrieved by the Partition outcome) might become aware of being implicitly offered a deal on the following lines. Stop provocations in Kashmir and on the Siachen Glacier. Emphasize rigorously the democratic and constitutional traditions in public life. In return, the much larger entity will look after your defence much more safely and securely and at much less expense to yourselves. (There will be no need to keep India's forces diverted by permanent confrontation; and, after all, your comparatively small nuclear force makes nonsense in the absence of a threat from India.) The union will also use its moral influence, and whatever conciliatory machinery is available (the UN's or its own), to address Pakistan/ Muslim grievances over Kashmir. Pakistan would be balancing the huge gain in security and in the reduced cost of military preparations against the loss of the forlorn hope of changing the Kashmir settlement by military force.

This is an offer, surely, that cannot be completely ignored. We have supposed that a country can accept it but continue at the same time to fly its flag and to have the symbols and trappings of statehood and some continuing international role, and also to exercise its own choice on all domestic policy issues that do not challenge union conventions and policies on such matters as the global environment, human rights and the rule of law. And any lowish-income country will be likely, simply through membership of the larger union, to receive economic benefits over and above the big reduction in security cost.

India would also gain hugely by Pakistan's accession under these conditions to the large entity. The immense cost of military confrontation would be removed, to say nothing of the risk. The next big question is whether it too, in this new situation, would have enough of an incentive to join the union – given what it would have to surrender and what to gain. One of the costs, as it might see them, would be the obligation it would implicitly be accepting of allowing Kashmir and similar grievances to come before the independent tribunal. But India might well feel weak and vulnerable and overstretched in relation to China, just as we have imagined that Pakistan had felt weak and vulnerable in relation to India. If so, the ayes might have it. India could still be the next domino.

Each accession in this way could represent potentially a gain in security, and a reduction in the cost of defence, both to the one that joins and to its neighbours. The union will be highly diverse in the emotional attachments of its member populations and states. If it remains democratic in those circumstances, it can be overwhelmingly on balance a protection and reassurance without being a threat. It will be too prudent to attack other than in defence of its peoples or under extreme provocation. It will be too powerful for its members to be subject to wanton official attack. The rules of accession will of course insist that, on a reasonable interpretation, each new member is demo-cratic and law-governed, and each will be accepting the authority of the Convention and Commission and Court of Human Rights, and the procedural rules and arbitral decisions of the tribunal we have pos-tulated on borders and cultural autonomy.

Is it really possible that both sides in a regional confrontation can gain from the fact that one of them has chosen to join a multinational union that has no emotional stakes in regional disputes? In terms of resource costs and physical security, the answer is definitely yes. On those computable measures, the union we have postulated can offer a markedly positive-sum deal to the regional powers. The potential *costs* to those powers are the non-computable ones of emotional allegiances and prestige. How far these count is a matter of perceptions: the way they are seen and presented. Accepting the scrutiny and authority of tribunals (on borders and cultural autonomy, and on human civil rights) may perhaps come to seem honourable dealing, rather than craven surrender, if the big powers of Europe, and possibly Russia (dare we speculate, even the United States, independently?) have been prepared to subject themselves to those same tribunals.

On the way ... risks of a four-superpower world

We are imagining, by say 2020 or 2025, the existence of a confederation, with the institutions of a democratic government, that centrally controls military policy and defence-related foreign policy; obliges member-states to allow submission of territorial and cultural-autonomy grievances to a process involving either legal decision or conciliation and arbitration; enforces human rights as a last resort within its members' territory; plays a decisive role in cross-member-state-border environmental issues; and responds to urgent demands for relief of distress and the promotion of economic and social 'development' that come through its political processes. It also oversees an area of free trade. It extends over almost all of Europe, including Turkey, Ukraine, and Russia – a population of some 750 to 800 million people – with possibly a few states from Southern Africa or elsewhere also belonging.

Simultaneously there is probably a free-trade area covering the Americas, and just possibly some separate political integration there. Elsewhere too (South-east Asia perhaps, the South-west Pacific) there might be regional groups of states each of which had developed some elements of a joint political structure. The more 'successful' the European Union appeared to be, the more its example, including some of its particular institutional arrangements, are likely to be copied.

On matters of war and peace the Union will probably have tried to maintain an equal and qualified partnership with the US, possibly still under the auspices of NATO.

The diversity of national traditions within the Union will tend to make it hesitant about warlike action: experience in 2002 and 2003 suggests a prevailing reluctance on the part of the population of the present Union to fight in dubious causes or without broad-based inter-national approval. At the time of writing, this widespread reluctance has been very evident: strong even among some of its peoples whose governments (such as those of Spain and Italy) have been committed to support of war against Saddam's Iraq. The Union as we have pic-tured it will be too big for most others to challenge aggressively, and at the same time too moderate to react rashly. Because of its inter-nal diversity, it may well be under less suspicion of vested interests or partisan motives in its foreign policy than large powers with strong national bases have normally been.

At the time we are considering, the four top military powers are likely to be China, India, the US, and the Union. The risk is that, among these four, some may see each other as enemies or potential enemies; be seen as enemies by smaller powers (Pakistan, Taiwan, Iran, North Korea); side with smaller powers against other smaller powers or against each other; themselves commit acts (possibly in areas they regard as their own territory) that give occasion for moral outrage; or move, without general enough approval, to right or to avenge such acts committed by others.

Unless China's dispute with Taiwan is settled, and unless and until it manages to avoid policies in minority areas that risk outraging the rest of the world, there is a possibility of an arms race between China and the US, with China a much more equal contestant than at present. Similar risks – though possibly not directly involving a second superpower in each case – are likely to arise if tension between the US and the Arab and Muslim worlds over Israel–Palestine, and between India and Pakistan over Kashmir, are not resolved. These three tragic legacies of the 1940s have persisted for over fifty years and may well continue for another fifty.

There are plenty of risks inherent in the existence of four, possibly roughly equal, large nuclear powers – with probably even more additional smaller nuclear powers, concentrated of course around trouble spots, than there are today. On the whole, however, the postulated advent of the Union as the fourth power – large and possibly well-armed, but extremely cautious and with no particular shared grievances and hates, replacing (among many others) two or three former veto-wielding nuclear states, firmly in the democratic camp but big enough not to be anybody's poodle – would be a positive element. Four superpowers, with such a union one of the four, seem likely to form a system intrinsically safer than the postulated alternative (in which the European Union has no more of an integrated foreign and defence policy than at present): probably three (the US, China, and India), with an independent nuclear-armed (perhaps still semi-humiliated) Russia a possible fourth, and France and Britain each independent and nuclear but neither counting for very much on its own.

Yet the aim must be, as soon as possible, to incorporate the four or so giants in a single union, for which, it might be hoped, the enlarged European-plus union would provide the template and working framework.

Of course, joining up with China or India would be a very different matter from joining up with Latvia. A superpower cannot be expected necessarily to be willing to fit into the Union constitution as it happens to be at the time, with no questions asked. Negotiation for confederation with other very big powers is likely to involve some institutional give-and-take.

From the viewpoint of the union developed from the EU there could be three types of obstacle to incorporation with any one of the others: the other's own reluctance to join; its internal characteristics; and its external disputes.

Against the first and second type of obstacle, the union could simply make itself as attractive as possible, especially being scrupulous to preserve the autonomies of its member-states in all matters not essential to union responsibility. Making the union attractive would encourage the reforms that could render postulant-members acceptable. And keeping the union open to any state that matched its entry criteria could lead to the impression of a bandwagon, as more and more states brought themselves to a condition in which they met the entry conditions, and its offer of admittance was progressively taken up by more and more postulants.

For the third type of obstacle, the remedy is, by all possible means, to clear up the critical disputes, principally the three fifty-year-old survivors already mentioned. Israel–Palestine ranges popular feeling right across the Arab and Islamic countries against the US, to the extent, in the most recent time, of provoking irrational and self-defeating responses on both sides. The relevance of the other two disputes is obvious. The time to settle is now, when there is only one hyperpower; when its interest, considered objectively, is strongly in favour of settling the one that most affects itself, which it could fairly readily do if it chose; and when, in combination with the rest of the 'West', it probably has large potential bargaining-pieces for dealing with the other two.

To draw the three or four potential superpowers of the second quarter of the century into a single confederation: that has to be the aim. Once it happens under something like the form we have supposed, the rest is likely to fall gradually more or less into place. Integration could surely become the fashion. An extended and open union springing from Europe, one that is already itself a real superpower through its military- and foreign-policy integration, can at least clear a way through which this may be possible. It shows a new model, and creates a new framework, of world organization that others can join without losing identity or dignity.

A European Union that is on principle purely and exclusively European, or a Union that does not have a confederally controlled defence and defence-related foreign policy, or one that tries to do *too much else* centrally, will either fail to provide the framework or fail to provide the model. It will be forgoing the most historic of historic opportunities.

It could well be that – no matter what the give-and-take – China, India, or the United States might not take up the opportunity even if it were offered on the best possible terms: the opportunity of a change of international system. Lack of imagination among leaders or the public, the self-interest of politicians, familiar chauvinist rhetoric, inertia: a combination of these elements might mean that we retained a world of four or so nuclear superpowers and an increasing number of other potentially lethal states.

What I am arguing is that we can envisage a situation in which the offer of a new, much safer, much less hate- and fear-absorbed world order is effectively and plausibly open. And we can envisage a set of moves – varying at only a few crucial points from what might be generally considered most likely to happen in any case – through which the process of bringing that world order into being might be set in motion.

It is for the members of the European Union to make those few crucial changes in the sequence. Then, for all the obstacles and hazards, there will be natural processes favouring the rest of the agenda.

Summary of Chapter 7

- Optimum routes may not be available in practice. But, insofar as there is a choice, the Union should proceed, as soon as possible, to create the machinery for a genuinely common defence and (defence-related) foreign policy. This would be of advantage to the world in the immediate future, quite apart from the long-term possibilities that it would open.

- Such a common policy will not come into being without genuinely confederal governmental institutions for defining and implementing it. This will require a democratically based Union Parliament and Executive to have real governmental powers, at least over this one all-important area of authority. According to the style of democratic institutions prevalent in Europe, this would probably mean an Executive effectively appointed by, and responsible to, the popularly elected chamber of Parliament: institutions that could be developed, with only a few key changes, from present EU governing bodies.

- The member-states could still participate autonomously and individually in those international agencies and forums not solely concerned with war-and-peace-related matters or trade restrictions. They could retain their identifiable military units within a Union force, and, given Union assent, deploy these at their discretion on peacekeeping or humanitarian missions.

- Entry conditions should, as soon as possible, include a full commitment to the procedures and decisions of a (Union or UN) tribunal set up to implement a convention for dealing with border disputes and claims for self-determination and cultural autonomy.

- Provided entry conditions can be fulfilled, the Union, after the ten new entries in 2004, might expect with moderate confidence to include the remainder of south-eastern Europe and Turkey by 2010 or soon after. If that expansion went well, it might hope, in the century's second decade, that Ukraine and Russia would come to be both eligible and willing to join. Both of these might, in the sequence imagined, find entry sufficiently attractive, especially if the Union already had a common defence and core-foreign policy so that it was a major power in world affairs. The Union might also, in this period or before, declare itself in principle open to any nation that fulfilled its entry conditions, and possibly seek actively to include any then-eligible or near-eligible state from Africa.

● There is reason to think that the resulting Union, possibly one of four superpowers by 2025, would act as a stabilizing element in world affairs on account of the combination of its size and weight with its lack of particular national historic resentments and competitive aspirations.

● Where two states were locked in a dangerous dispute, large net advantages *to both* would arise if one of them were to join the Union.

● The hope would be that eventually the other superpowers might come *both to see the advantages* of joining together in the kind of framework embodied in the Union *and to meet the requirements* of acceptable partnership – with or without some further changes in Union institutions. To this end, every effort should be devoted to settling the three (now fifty-year-old) disputes that bedevil the international relations of the US, China, and India.

● Much depends on the Union's readiness now to make the few key changes that would leave it an open flexible association but also allow it to become a force to be reckoned with. On those terms it can be an instrument for moving to a safer and more just world order.

Note

1. Any possibility that Russian incorporation into the Union may frighten China and add dangerous instability to Russian–Chinese relations should be reduced if the Union is already a single power for defence purposes when Russia joins. China will in that case know that, *first*, it will not be attacked from the Russian side on account of purely Russian preoccupations; and, *second*, attacking Russia would be attacking a much bigger and more powerful adversary than Russia alone. Incorporation of Russia even into a Union that is not yet a single defence unit might also on balance serve to calm relations with China through weaker manifestations of the same effects, though there must be elements of uncertainty in this case.

Chapter 8

Résumé and challenge

The argument recapitulated

It is of the utmost importance that we should find a sustainable system for maintaining peace, consistent with no loss of security against attack or forceful domination, and with at worst no sacrifice of the rudimentary elements of civil and social justice.

The need for peace, in a form consistent with security and justice, is paramount in a world that has abundant potential occasions for warfare, unofficial and official. The urgency of this need is enhanced by the immensely destructive character of modern military technology, the tendency for more and more states to acquire nuclear weapons, and the incentives for not only governments but also irregulars to obtain both these and other weapons of mass destruction.

There is unlikely to be any satisfactory long-term solution to the problem of preserving peace short of bringing official military forces under a single government-type authority. Such an authority would not be tolerable, and for that reason would not be attainable, unless it was set up under a democratic and law-governed constitutional order with safeguards against the tyranny of the majority.

Reaching that outcome by the most direct route may take thirty or fifty years, or even longer, but the inevitable delay only emphasizes the importance of starting consciously and explicitly to work towards it now. This demands some rough picture of the goal and of the process by which it may be reached. Decisions taken now may facilitate or impede its attainment.

Alternative devices for preserving peace turn out to be uncertainly achievable, or widely unacceptable, or else dubiously effective even if achieved. Examples are reliance on a single but overwhelmingly powerful, righteous hyperpower to determine matters at its discretion; maintaining through alliances, and through pragmatic and morally neutral respect for each other's 'interests', a stable balance among a number of large but more-or-less co-equal powers and alliances; forming a large alliance of independent but likeminded states committed to collective security; and regulating international relations by a purely consensual system of international law and tribunals. Because of the inevitable delay before any satisfactory system of government-type global control can be reached, however, other approaches must be applied in the meantime. The alternative approaches are not all necessarily inconsistent with the processes needed to work towards governmental military union. In particular the attempt to establish consensually a law-simulating order in international relations should simultaneously be vigorously pursued. The quest for peace has to be both short-term and long-term.

The fact that much fighting involves unofficial forces, on one side or both, does not diminish the importance of the objective of global control of official military forces. But it does increase the relevance of other possible functions of a global or near-global authority that might reduce the grievances that lead to civil conflict. That authority should be associated with an *obligatory* regime for the submission of disputes over borders or cultural autonomy to a conciliatory and arbitral procedure. We should also move as far as we can in the meantime to achieve a *consensual* regime with the same functions.

Beside the control of military forces, and authority to impose the dispute procedure, there are global powers required for the sake of other aspects of security and justice. The global union would need to have a power, concurrent with that of member-states but able to override it, over environmental matters that cross state borders, and the power to respond to social disasters and emergencies such as those that may result from environmental change. It would need to have the authority to enforce an investigatory and judicial regime for the protection of civil rights. And it would need the financial powers that would enable it to carry out these functions and progressively to move toward the ideal of rudimentary social justice within its domain.

Peace, certain aspects of environmental security, civil justice, and social justice: these can all be regarded as examples of *global public-goods* in the broad sense, goods that individual states are unlikely to be able to secure to the necessary degree without at least co-ordination. The special character of these particular public-goods – principally the sacrifices of various kinds (of economic resources, power, or elements of self-image and favoured symbols) that would have to be made for the sake of securing them – means that, in order to be reliably secured, they are likely to require governmental, and not merely consensual ('intergovernmental'), institutions of global management. However, as with the pursuit of peace, every effort should be made *now* to come as close as possible to the satisfactory delivery of these and other global public-goods through consensual institutions, mainly those of the United Nations family. A number of specific developments are mooted.

The path to a governmental union with the essential functions mentioned will be eased by working explicitly towards the form of union here characterized as a confederation: one that any member-state may, through defined constitutional procedures, leave if its people so decide. It will also be eased if uniformity or central powers are not prescribed where they are not essential. There are important global public-goods (such as economic stabilization, plugging tax loopholes, and regulation of transnational business) that can effectively be provided without global *governmental* institutions. This is because they can readily be generated by devices through which the general public of virtually every country can benefit, even in the short term. There are also other functions commonly controlled centrally in federal states that do not need to be provided by global institutions at all.

Since it is evident that global confederation must come through the voluntary decision of states to join together, and since in each country there is likely in advance to be great uncertainty over the effects of surrender of state powers, and over the extent to which accommodation with other states is possible, the process of formation can come about only through a gradual process of progressive *widening* (admitting new members) and *deepening* (expanding the range of authority of union institutions and intensifying the union element, as distinct from the intergovernmental element, in this authority).

What is now the European Union has been engaged in this process for over forty years and thus provides a *model* of how it can be done. It also provides, on certain key conditions, a potential *vehicle* through which the required form of global union can be gradually approached. Advantageous for this purpose is the fact that most of its neighbour countries have been keen to join it.

The key conditions required for the Union to serve as a means of transport toward global confederation are, first, that it should abandon any requirement that its members must be European states, and, second, that certain aspirations to unity and openness or to uniformity within the Union should be either abandoned or left as optional extras in which member-states may or may not choose to participate. Aspects of the present European Union's application of, and aspirations to, uniformity or internal openness that would need to be made optional or negotiable for members include the single currency and monetary control, and completely free internal movement of labour. Anything much like the existing system of uniform farm support would also have to go.

On balance it would seem best that the form of constitutional democracy devised for the confederation should be a variant of the 'Westminster' system, in which a legislature, or the predominant chamber of the legislature, is elected in rough proportion to population and the executive is effectively chosen by that legislature or chamber, is responsible to it, and under certain conditions may be dismissed by it. Because of the desirability, or even necessity, in the circumstances likely to exist in a global confederation, for checks on the majority, it is proposed that, on financial measures and measures for the appointment of the executive, the legislature or predominant chamber should vote by 'houses' (each consisting of the representatives of a group of member-countries, the group self-selected by the countries' representatives under constraints imposed to limit the number of such houses), so that a sufficiently large majority in any house voting against would suffice to veto the measure. At the same time, to ensure continuity of government, the legislature's failure to pass a budget or to choose an executive should be met by constitutional provisions for previous financial measures to be effectively continued or for the previous executive to remain in office. If there is an 'upper' legislative chamber representing governments of member-states, one that might represent smaller members more heavily than their weight in total population would dictate, it might be empowered, by a sufficiently large majority, to delay for reconsideration – or, in certain defined cases, by a particularly large majority, to override – decisions of the popularly elected chamber. (Also, by a very large majority, it might be entitled to override the 'house veto' proposed above, in favour of the majority decision in the popular chamber.)

The European Union could move toward these arrangements by broadly continuing its general trend of giving increasing power to the European Parliament as against the member-governments, and reducing the extent to which individual member-governments can block decisions. Moves recently suggested (the former of them in the draft Constitution) whereby the President of the Council would be elected by the Council for a period of years, and the President of the Commission would be elected by the Parliament alone, could provide a convenient transition. The President of the Council might evolve into the equivalent of a non-executive, umpire-type head of state, and the President of the Commission into a more conventional chief executive, who would come to choose other members of the executive subject (possibly) to the Parliament's approval. The Parliament could evolve into the predominant lower chamber and the Council into a revising and delaying, and *in extremis* blocking, upper chamber. Representation in the Parliament, and (as proposed in the current draft Constitution) voting-power in the Council, would need to be fixed according to rational formulas, so that they would not have to be negotiated afresh each time new members entered the Union.

The Union (as again in the draft Constitution) might regularize arrangements under which certain functions that some but not all members wished to run in common – as now happens with the common currency – could be managed by the Union's institutions. There would need to be a procedure for any member-state to leave the Union on condition of a sufficiently firm choice to that effect by the people of that state. This would include guidelines and routines for allotting the seceding state a share in the official assets and liabilities of the union, and particularly for clarifying the claims it might have over military assets. As is evident, elements of these prescriptions for Union development appear in the constitutional proposals approved by the Inter-Governmental Conference in June 2004.

The Union's entry conditions would have to be modified to drop any requirement that entrants should be European, and to change the way in which the Union's aspirations were expressed (for example, not to include 'economic and monetary union' as a universal commitment). Otherwise they could remain very much as they are: the four basic political tests; a system sufficiently market-oriented to fit with the Union's market rules; and implicitly evidence of some degree of political and economic stability. The political tests particularly should be rigorously applied. But, so long as those conditions were not compromised, the Union should in the next decade or two welcome or even actively seek the incorporation of the two extremely important states extending geographically from Europe into Asia, namely Turkey and Russia. At some time in the same period it might explicitly state its willingness in principle to admit states in any part of the world that could meet its entry conditions. The desire of states to join might in fact have the effect of shifting them toward satisfying the political tests of democracy, rule-of-law, human rights, and protection of minorities. There has already been evidence of such an effect.

For both long-term and short-term reasons, it is important that the Union should move as soon as possible toward having a genuinely common defence policy and defence-related foreign policy. It is almost inevitable that this will require the pooling of all members' military forces under a single authority and that the authority should be a single constitutional executive responsible to a single popularly elected legislative chamber. If the Union, despite inevitable divergence of opinion among its people and governments, is to be able to speak, negotiate, and act as an entity in matters of peace and war, it must have, even if only for the purpose of controlling this one function, a constitutional democratic government.

Movement *fairly soon* to that position is important to the long-term project set forward here. It is likely to be easier to follow a sequence in which a limited number of small and medium-sized states agree *first* to form a defence confederation large enough to constitute a top-rank power, and *then* seek to attract the rest of the world, including crucially important large states such as Russia, than to attract the large states first and then to proceed to a government-type defence union.

But transforming the European Union into a single entity for defence and defence-related purposes also has the potential for making the Union into a more effective force for peace and justice in the near future and broadly for fulfilling the objectives of its people and governments. This has become much more evident as a result of the international events that have taken place since the latter part of the year 2001.

The people and governments of the present Union are broadly with the United States in wanting to promote and maintain democracy, the rule of law, and a liberal order across the world. Many of them have found themselves since 2001 opposed to the forces within the present United States government that would ignore, downgrade, and even destroy, international law and international institutions. Until 2001, for half a century, Western Europe's areas of agreement with the US had been clearly more important than its areas of opposition. This is no longer necessarily the case. Over the Iraq issue, almost inevitably, the major governments of the Union pulled in different directions in response to the dilemma. Consequently the countries of the Union counted for little in exercising the restraint which, as far as we can judge, most of the people in the Union as it then was wished to apply. Grandstanding, appeals to national prejudice, the complications arising from the various actors' domestic politics, honest differences in judgement, created a divided voice.

The Union of 2004 has a much larger population than that of the US and an income of the same order. Potentially it is a comparable power. Inclusion of Turkey, Ukraine, and Russia would greatly increase that potential. At the same time, because of its diversity, it would still as an entity be free from the historical and dogmatic prejudices and hang-ups that commonly beset nations, even the other great powers of today and the near future. It would not have any predisposition to be pro- or anti- Christian or Jewish or Muslim or Orthodox or Slav or Hindu or secularist. It would be a force for moderation, weighty enough not to be ignored, able to give discriminating support to its partner across the Atlantic.

Four key requests to the European Union now

1. Take seriously the commitment to a common security and foreign policy, and move toward the necessary institutions, which are those of working constitutional democracy.

2. Allow freedom of labour movement to be negotiable.

3. Allow certain elements of common action – notably at the moment the common currency and monetary control – to be explicitly optional.

4. Keep open the possibility of accession for countries beyond Europe that meet the political entry conditions.

The first request is for fulfilling an aspiration unanimously agreed by member-governments as early as 1991. The second would remove a political obstacle to accessions, even perhaps some already in the queue. The third and fourth involve acknowledging in principle what is already part-accepted in practice. In sum, take the Union's most ambitious aspiration seriously; check the passion for uniformity; and let the gates that are open stay open.

Produce the counter-arguments

This book will be justified if it at least raises these issues and has them rationally discussed. It may be that it is a mistake to think that there is no reliable security for the world in submitting to the decisions of an unrestrained hyperpower with a democratic ideology but powerful religious, communal and industrial lobbies; or in the balance of power; or in collective security among independent powers; or in international law and institutions as they now are. But let that position be argued.

It may be that there is a fundamental scientific law implying that the military forces of the world can never be controlled by a single authority, or at least by a single democratic authority. Any public-house philosopher will tell you that for nothing (regardless of the fact that, for example, India today, democratic on balance whatever its faults, keeps under a single authority the armaments of a population of the same order as that of the whole world in 1850). But is it necessarily so?

It may be that advancing a strategy – however gradual – for moving by assent toward a world confederation over a few key functions would actually make the world of today a more dangerous place. But why should that be the case?

It may be that a European Union including Russia would necessarily be controlled by Russia – just as tabloid journalists in 1990 needed no convincing that the Union would be controlled by a united Germany – despite the plain implications of the relevant arithmetic. But do these apprehensions really add up?

Pub philosophers and tabloid journalists can assert any number of impossibilities and inevitabilities, just as people of all ages and both sexes can relate any number of old wives' tales. But, just as we don't credit every old wives' tale, we should have learned by now to be sceptical over alleged political impossibilities and inevitabilities.

It may be that the European Union would really serve the world better by shutting the gates and pulling up the drawbridge against Turks, infidels, and heretics; against those peoples some of which have provided the moral icons among the politicians of the twentieth century – against the Indians once mobilized by Gandhi, against the South Africans recently led by Mandela; against the nation that has given us Tolstoy and Dostoyevsky in case we are contaminated by Mongol hordes. It may be that the Union would more effectively contribute to peace and security by remaining simply a forum on international policy among the governments of a handful of small and medium states and providing cover for a few modest military operations to which some of its members contributed jointly – rather than by taking steps to turn itself into a major power. It may be that talking about a common defence and foreign policy is much safer and more satisfying than doing anything about it. But let the case be made.

A race for survival

If we survive the present century without some human-made disaster of vast proportions (the most likely candidate still being a nuclear war), then probably we shall have found some way by the year 2100 of pooling and jointly controlling armaments – and maybe running in common one or two other ventures in which we need to act together. It will probably be because we have found that solution that we have survived – even more so if we have survived without a much-magnified repeat of the slaughter of the first half of the twentieth century.

If slaughter-free survival is an overriding requirement, then perhaps the question should be not *whether we should seek*, but *by what means and how soon we can reach*, a global confederation in control of armed forces. To win the survival race, if that is what it is, we need three ingredients: a rough practical vision of the route, a sense of urgency, and patience.

We need patience because the target will not be reached in a day. For this same reason, we need a sense of urgency: a coherent start to the course cannot come a moment too soon. And we need at least a rough picture of the route, so that we know which way to go.

But is it the right vehicle?

Getting to the goal on time may be a matter of life and death. There is a vintage tractor standing by that just might serve, with careful steering, to make the journey. It has been repeatedly patched up but still works. Why it was procured in the first place is a matter of dispute; but there is a strong contrary view now that it should simply be restored for display.

The real year of manufacture is also doubtful. The documents appear to say 1957, but some enthusiasts believe that the modernized 1787 model is the only one worth restoring for either admiration or use. We have a choice between cleaning and polishing it and replacing its dented bodywork until it is a thing of beauty and the admiration of all – or else preparing it as well as we can to withstand the actual road it has to travel and starting it up without delay in its present battered state, driving it along a way that is only partly mapped, and doing impromptu repairs when they are necessary to keep it mobile: all with the aim of reaching that crucial goal in time.

The tractor is not the ideal piece of equipment for the journey. It would be aesthetically more satisfying as a carefully maintained show-piece. But it is the only vehicle around that may just prove suitable for the terrain. For all its faults, for all the uncertainties of the venture, it is more likely to get us there than any available alternative.

Without a sense of urgency, without patience, or without a rough idea of the way, we would never attempt the road. It is tempting to take an easy way out: to let the vehicle be used for what many take to be its proper function, as a museum specimen.

But there is that little matter of life and death.

Bibliography

Amnesty 99. January–February 2000.

Atkinson, Anthony B., ed. 2004. *New Sources for Development Finance*. Oxford: Oxford University Press.

Avi-Yonah, Reuven. 2000. 'Globalization, Tax Competition, and the Fiscal Crisis of the Welfare State'. *Harvard Law Review* 113: 1575–1676.

Bainbridge, Timothy. 2002. *The Penguin Companion to European Union*. 3rd edn. London: Penguin.

Barrett, Scott. 1999. 'Montreal versus Kyoto: International Co-operation and the Global Environment'. In Inge Kaul, Isabelle Grunberg, and Marc A. Stern, eds, *Global Public Goods: International Cooperation in the 21st Century*, New York and Oxford: Oxford University Press: 192–219.

Baumert, K., R. Bandari and N. Kete. 1999. *What Might a Developing Country Commitment Look Like?* Washington DC: World Resources Institute. Cited Grubb et al. 1999: 263 note.

BIS [Bank for International Settlements]. 2001. 71st Annual Report, 2000–1. Basel: BIS.

Bobbitt, Philip. 2002. *The Shield of Achilles*. London: Allen Lane.

Boughton, James. 2001. *Quiet Revolution: the International Monetary Fund 1979–1989*. Washington DC: IMF.

Cecil, David. 1955. *Melbourne*. London: The Reprint Society, by arrangement with Constable & Co.

Childers, Erskine, and Brian Urquhart. 1994. *Renewing the United Nations System*. Uppsala: Dag Hammarskjöld Foundation.

Clark, Peter B., and Jacques J. Polak. 2002. 'International Liquidity and the Role of the SDR in the International Monetary System'. IMF Working Paper No. 02/217. Washington DC: IMF.

Clunies-Ross, Anthony. 2000. 'Untying the Knots of International Environmental Agreements'. *Journal of Economic Studies* 27 (1/2): 94–110.

Clunies-Ross, Anthony. 2003. 'Resources for Social Development'. Paper for the World Commission on the Social Dimension of Globalization. Geneva: ILO. Available at: www.ilo.org/wcsdg

Cooper, Robert, 1996. *The Post-Modern State*. London: Demos.

Council of Europe. 2004. *The European Convention on Human Rights and its Five Protocols*. Hellenic Resources Network Inc. Available at: http://www.hri.org/docs/ECHR50.html.

Devarajan, Shantayanan, Margaret J. Miller and Eric V. Swanson. 2002. 'Goals for Development: History, Prospects and Costs'. World Bank Policy Research Working Paper, wps 2819, April 2002. Washington DC: World Bank.

The Economist, 18.1.2003: 41; 21.6.2003: 23–5; 26.6.2004: 12.

European Parliament. 2004. *Summary of the Constitution adopted by the European Council in Brussels on 17/18 June 2004*. Brussels: European Parliament Delegation to the Convention, Secretariat. Found at: www.cec.org.uk, by following 'Index A–Z' and thence 'Constitution'.

European Union. 2003. Report of the Future of Europe Convention. Draft Treaty establishing a Constitution for Europe, adopted by consensus by the European Convention on 13 June and 10 July 2003. Submitted to the President of the European Council in Rome on 18 July 2003. Available at: http://europa.eu.int/futurum/constitution/declaration/finalact_en.htm (accessed 22 Febrauary 2005)

European Union. 2004. Draft Treaty Establishing a Constitution for Europe, as presented by the Conference of the Representatives of the Governments of the Member States, 18 June 2004. Here compiled from documents cig 50/03, cig 81/04, cig 85/04, found at www.cec.org.uk by following 'Index A-Z' and thence 'Constitution'.

Felix, David. 2001. 'Annual Revenue from a Tobin Tax under Alternative Tax Rates'. Conference papers, Halifax Initiative Conference on Taxing Currency Transactions: from Feasibility to Implementation. Vancouver, 4–6 October 2001: 39–47.

Grubb, Michael, with Christiaan Vrolijk and Duncan Brack. 1999. *The Kyoto Protocol: a Guide and Assessment*. London: Earthscan and Royal Institute of International Affairs.

Grubb, Michael. 2000. 'Economic Dimensions of Technological and Global Responses to the Kyoto Protocol'. *Journal of Economic Studies* 27 (1/2): 111–25.

International Financial Statistics Yearbook. 2002. Washington DC: IMF.

Kagan, Robert. 2002. 'Atlantic Crossing'. In *AFR Weekend Review*, 23.8.2002. Reprinted from *Prospect*; an edited version of a longer article that appeared in *Policy Review*, the journal of the Hoover Institution (www.policyreview.org).

Keesing [*Keesing's Record of World Events*].

Kissinger, Henry. 1995. *Diplomacy*. New York: Touchstone Book, Simon and Schuster.

Knightley, Phillip, and Peter Pringle. 1992. 'At Daggers Drawn'. *The Independent*, 6.10.1992: 19.

Lomborg, Bjørn. 2001. *The Skeptical Environmentalist: Measuring the Real State of the World*. Cambridge: Cambridge University Press.

Lowenson, Richard, and Alan Whiteside. 2001. 'HIV/AIDS: Implications for Poverty Reduction'. Background paper prepared for the United Nations Development Programme for the United Nations General Assembly Special Session on HIV/AIDS, 25–27 June 2001.

Maritain, Jacques. 1954. *Man and the State*. London: Hollis and Carter.

Mussa, Michael. 1996. 'Is there a Case for Allocation under the Present Articles?' In Michael Mussa et al. *Exchange Rate Regimes in an Increasingly Integrated World Economy*. IMF Occasional Paper 193. Cited Clark and Polak 2002.

Ostrom, Elinor. 1990. *Managing the Commons*. Cambridge: Cambridge University Press.

Rees, Martin. 2003. *Our Final Century*. London: Heinemann.

Roberts, Andrew. 2000. *Salisbury: Victorian Titan*. London: Phoenix.

Sandler, Todd. 1997. *Global Challenges: an Approach to Environmental, Political and Economic Problems*. Cambridge: Cambridge University Press.

Schmidt, Rodney. 1999. 'A Feasible Foreign Exchange Transactions Tax'. Paper presented to the North-South Institute, Ottawa, June 1999.

Schmidt, Rodney. 2001. 'Efficient Capital Controls'. *Journal of Economic Studies* 28 (3): 199–212.

Soros, George. 2002. *On Globalization*. Oxford: Public Affairs.

Spahn, Paul-Bernd. 1996. 'The Tobin Tax and Exchange-Rate Stability'. *Finance and Development* 33 (June): 24–7.

Spahn, Paul-Bernd. 2002. *On the Feasibility of a Tax on Foreign Exchange Transactions*. Report to the Federal Ministry for Economic Co-operation and Development, Bonn, February 2002. Available at: www.wiwi.uni-frankfurt.de/professoren/spahn/tobintax

Tanzi, Vito. 1995. *Taxation in an Integrating World*. Washington DC: Brookings Institution.

Tanzi, Vito. 1996. 'Is there a Need for a World Tax Organization?' Paper prepared for presentation at the International Institute of Public Finance, 52nd Congress, Tel-Aviv, 28–29 August 1996.

The Times (London), 31.12.2002: 15.

UK Treasury and DfID [Department for International Development]. 2003. 'The International Finance Facility (IFF)'. Paper issued in January 2003.

UN. 2001. Report to the Secretary-General of the High Level Panel on Financing for Development [the Zedillo Report], 25 June 2001.

World Bank. 2000. *World Development Report 1999/2000*. Oxford: Oxford University Press for the World Bank.

World Bank. 2001. *Global Development Finance 2001*.

Wyplosz, Charles. 1999. 'International Financial Instability'. In Inge Kaul, Isabelle Grunberg and Marc A. Stern, eds, *Global Public Goods: International Cooperation in the 21st Century*. New York and Oxford: UNDP and Oxford University Press: 152–89.

Index

Index

Index

176